Teaching Children to Learn

Robert Fisher

STANLEY
THORNES

First published in 1995 by:
Stanley Thornes (Publishers) Ltd
Ellenborough House
Wellington Street
CHELTENHAM GL50 1YW
England

96 97 98 99 00 / 10 9 8 7 6 5 4 3 2

A catalogue record of this book is available from the British Library.

ISBN 0 7487 2091 X

Typeset by Merle & Alan Thompson
Creative Editing

Printed and bound in Great Britain at Redwood Books, Trowbridge, Wiltshire.

Contents

Introduction

I am still learning.
    Motto of Michaelangelo

My brain is like a massive forest. It's full of amazing ideas.
    Child, aged eleven

All human beings have a basic right to the full development of their minds and of their capacity for learning. There is a growing realisation that the development of individuals and of communities depends on education, and on the quality of teaching and learning. The needs of individuals and the needs of society meet in the need to develop lifelong and autonomous learners, students who value learning as an empowering activity, who want to learn independently and who have self-determination, self-direction and self-respect. We need to develop students who can effectively participate in society and meet the challenge of rapid social change. For teachers the challenge is – how do we foster the learning that will help achieve these goals?

In recent years there has been a world-wide explosion of interest into ways of developing thinking and learning. Research in and development of cognitive education is progressing rapidly in many countries. This book does not set out to be a comprehensive review of all the research into teaching children to learn. Rather it is intended to serve as a practical guide to ways of teaching that have been shown to develop effective learning.

Successful learners not only have a lot of knowledge, they also know how to learn. Research from many countries shows that certain teaching strategies are common to classrooms where effective learning takes place. We are now able to identify some of the kinds of teaching that will best help children to learn.

This book describes ten simple but powerful teaching strategies most closely linked to success in learning. These strategies can be applied to any field of learning, and are the processes most likely to achieve the goals of independent and effective learning. The ten teaching strategies that make up the chapters of this book aim to foster the expansion of thinking and learning throughout the curriculum. These are:

1 Thinking to learn

Learning is best developed through a 'thinking skills' approach, which aims to teach children not only what to learn but how to learn. This means offering challenges to thinking, and giving time for thinking, to students in all areas of their learning.

2 Questioning

A characteristic of effective learners is that they ask questions of themselves and of others. An enquiring classroom will both generate questions and encourage students to develop their own questions.

3 Planning

Research shows that those successful in any field tend to spend more time at the planning stage. For children, this means they need to know the value of planning, the skills of planning and to develop dispositions to follow a 'plan-do-review' process of learning.

4 Discussing

Children need to articulate their thinking and learning. Good teachers encourage interpretative discussion. They utilise 'think-pair-share', allowing individual thinking time, discussion with a partner, and then group or class discussion, creating in the classroom a community of enquiry.

5 Cognitive mapping

Concept mapping, also called 'mind mapping', helps children to articulate their thinking, converting the verbal into the visually memorable. Mapping helps children organise what they know, and to create new patterns of understanding.

6 Divergent thinking

All learning should allow for some personal expression and individual variation. We value what we have made our own. Divergent thinking means offering choices, encouraging individual responsibility and a creative response to learning.

7 Co-operative learning

Learning with a partner, sometimes called 'peer tutoring', or with a group can extend opportunities both for learning from and for teaching others. Children can benefit from working with less able, with more able and with similar-ability peers.

8 Coaching

Children need help in fulfilling their potential as thinkers and learners. In learning how to learn, children need teaching that includes cognitive coaching. Coaching can help to provide the cognitive structures that turn teaching into learning.

9 Reviewing

Children need time to review what they have done, to assess what they have learnt, and to draw out lessons or targets for the future. They also need positive feedback when it is honestly given and deserved. Feedback, and feedforward, make for future success.

10 Creating a learning community

Children need support for learning, from their environment at school, at home, and in the community. What are the characteristics of powerful

An overview chart

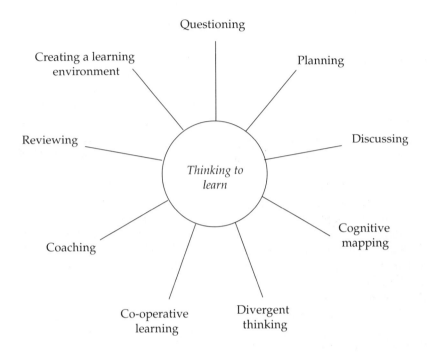

Questioning

Creating a learning
environment

Planning

Reviewing

Discussing

*Thinking to
learn*

Coaching

Cognitive
mapping

Co-operative
learning

Divergent
thinking

environments for teaching and learning? How do you create a learning community?

Included in each chapter are a number of tasks which are listed on the next page. These offer ways to explore the themes through teaching and learning activities with children. References are included at the end of each chapter and suggestions for further reading are given at the end of the book.

Teaching Children to Learn is not a recipe book that supplies easy answers. It seeks to offer a framework for a policy of active learning for any community, classroom or school. The process of improving teaching and learning, of developing the curriculum and assessing children's progress is a process of enquiry and research. If helping students to become more effective thinkers and learners is a valid goal of education, then this is a research project which involves us all.

Robert Fisher
Centre for Thinking Skills
Brunel University College

Table of tasks

1 Thinking to learn

How a thinking curriculum helps develop intelligence and learning

The basic ideas that lie at the heart of all disciplines are as simple as they are powerful. It is only when such ideas are put in formalised terms ... that they are out of reach of the young child.
Jerome Bruner

Isn't all education about helping us to think? Isn't that what we have a brain for?
Child, aged ten

Young children are powerful learners. They begin communicating with their mothers from birth by using their body language in a dance of gestures and smiles. Some researchers suggest that this communicating and learning process begins even earlier, in the womb. Pregnant women, aiming to maximise the learning potential of their child, can begin by talking, reading, singing and playing favourite music to their unborn baby. Many who do so report feeling unexpected responses!

From an early age, the thinking child learns to master the most demanding of learning tasks – the acquisition of language. Children bring into the world an amazing strength of curiosity, an elasticity of thought, and an ability to ask and respond to deep and challenging questions, like these from four-year olds: 'Why do people die?', 'What holds up the sky?', 'How does an oak tree fit inside an acorn?' This early curiosity often withers with the effects of ageing and schooling. As one child said: 'I like school. You don't have to think. They tell you what to do.' Keeping a child's early questioning spirit alive can be one of the keys to success in learning. So how do you do it? How do you encourage a thinking child?

One way is to introduce the child to complex and abstract ideas. This can begin at an early age. A surgeon, who was also a caring father, was keen to develop the learning skills of his young son. The doctor specialised in brain surgery so he decided to share his enthusiasm and knowledge with his three-year old. First, he named parts of the brain, pointing to his head, and then drew large simple coloured pictures. Soon the young boy could identify the cerebellum and the cortex, and was saying to visitors in a quizzical way: 'How's your head?' By the age of four, he had a better knowledge of parts of the brain than most adults, simply because the topic had been presented to him in a sophisticated, but simple, way by an enthusiastic adult.

All children are born with potential, and we cannot be sure of the learning limits of any child. Many children, however, including the very able and the 'strugglers', fail to fulfil their potential. The possible causes of educational failure and frustration are varied and often difficult to diagnose. Many causes, however, stem from what could be called 'cognitive confusion'.

Children suffer cognitive confusion when confronted with messages and demands which seem to make no sense. They are told to make a journey but they have no map. Children become confused and fail because of two broad factors:

- they cannot overcome blocks to learning
- they have not learnt how to learn.

Children need help to achieve their potential and to overcome the blocks to learning – the 'I don't know what to do', 'I can't do it' and 'I don't want to do it' responses – and to identify ways in which they can become effective learners – the 'I know what to do', 'I can do it (or at least try to do it)' and 'I want to try' attitudes. One way to begin thinking about learning is to try to identify what some of the blocks to learning might be.

> **TASK 1**
>
> **Identifying blocks to learning**
> What are some of the factors that can block learning?
> 1 Think about your own learning and consider the blocks you have experienced. It may be helpful to consider blocks to learning under three headings:
>   a) factors within yourself – why did you find it hard?
>   b) factors within the learning environment – what did not help you?
>   c) factors within the subject matter – why was that hard to learn?
> 2 Discuss with children what they find hard to learn, and why they find it hard. Can they identify any of the blocks to their learning?

An 11-year old, encouraged to think about what the blocks to his learning were, identified the following factors:

- in himself *boredom, hunger, sickness, dyslexia (when your brain doesn't work as fast as other people's), tiredness, and lack of interest*
- in the environment *flies buzzing, ink running out, the person next to me disturbing me (smashing my face in), no pen, no paper, no knowledge, and no life*
- in the subject *work is too hard, work is too long, work is illegible, no work to do, no subject (nothing to work on), and work does not interest me.*

All children are 'at potential' in their learning, with the capability of exploring many paths of experience, and of creating new paths to explore – as in the lines of Robert Frost:

> *Two roads diverged in a wood, and I –*
> *I took the one less travelled by,*
> *And that has made all the difference.*
>   from 'The Road Not Taken'

All children, whatever their ability, are also 'at risk' – of being bogged down in lower forms of thinking and of endlessly repetitive experience; of not seeing new paths; of not knowing how to travel thoughtfully; and of missing opportunities to explore fresh avenues of knowledge and experience. A good deal of research has gone into examining the differences between successful and less successful learners. What does this research suggest are the best ways of helping a child think and learn more effectively?

Traditionally there have been two approaches to teaching thinking and learning skills. One is to develop a specific programme to teach children thinking skills. The other is to teach thinking and learning skills through all areas of the curriculum. Let us look at these two approaches in more detail.

A specific programme …?

In the past, specific subjects have been identified as those that will develop the ability to learn. Latin was once said to be such a subject, but research in the 1920s by Thorndike found that pupils studying Latin showed no measurable cognitive advantages over similar sets of students not studying Latin. There was no transfer from the rigours of learning Latin grammar into higher levels of thinking in other subjects. Pupils who learnt Latin became good at Latin, and also knowledgeable about grammar, Roman history and the roots of several European languages, but this did not mean that they became better thinkers and learners in any general sense.

Mathematicians have claimed that mathematics is the true foundation for logic and good reasoning, but there is no evidence that mathematicians are better thinkers and learners than others in any general sense. Claims have been made that the computer programme LOGO can provide the cognitive tools for problem-solving,[1] but there is little evidence that such skills transfer to other areas of learning. Mathematics reflects an important aspect of intelligence, but not all the modes needed for effective thinking. The same may be said for teaching the formal rules of logic. But what of science? Is that not the queen of subjects, as it includes mathematics, logic and all forms of thinking about the real world?

Scientific method underpins much of modern progress, and recent research into science education suggests that children's general cognitive development can be enhanced though a particular approach to science education. This research is called the Cognitive Acceleration through Science Education project (CASE).[2] This aims to help students of 11–14 years to draw out certain key scientific principles such as fair testing, probability and classification, by focusing on these in the discussion of scientific experiments. This drawing out of the principles that underlies scientific reasoning – the key concepts of rational investigation, helps students to transfer these principles into other areas of learning. Research shows that general levels of success can be raised through specific programmes aimed at developing children's thinking and learning skills.

There are many programmes aimed at developing thinking skills.

- Creative thinking courses, such as Edward de Bono's CoRT materials.
- Philosophy programmes, such as those devised by Matthew Lipman.

- Instrumental enrichment (IE) programmes devised by Reuven Feuerstein and his associates.

Over 200 such programmes have been developed (mainly in America). But the big question remains: do the skills they aim to develop improve the student's ability to think and learn? The evidence for this is positive, but rather thin. What the evidence does show is that teachers who are enthusiastic and well trained in a programme produce good results. Teachers who are less keen and less certain about the value of what they are doing produce variable results. The message from research seems to be that programmes focusing on developing thinking skills can work, and, in the hands of good teachers, do work. They show that you can teach children to think and reason more effectively and bring greater success in learning.

...or thinking across the curriculum?

Another approach is to infuse the teaching of thinking skills into all aspects of the curriculum. This is achieved through involving children in active learning situations that extend their higher order thinking processes. In developing thinking across the curriculum, two of the questions that need to be asked are as follows.

- What are the higher forms of thinking that students should be engaged in?
- What learning activities or approaches will develop the higher order thinking?

According to research by Bloom,[3] lower levels of thinking involve knowledge (knowing the facts), comprehension (understanding the facts), and application (applying the facts). Higher levels involve analysis (taking the facts apart), synthesis (creating something new from the facts), and finally evaluation (evaluating the knowledge). These levels are said to represent the growing complexity and challenge to a child's thinking about any particular topic (see page 18).

The learning child is a thinking child. Successful learning involves helping children to move on to higher levels of thinking. These higher levels are characterised by what has been called 'metacognitive control'. Thinking can be seen as an information-processing capacity that involves input, output and control. It is through the exercise of control that higher levels of thinking can be developed (see Figure 1.1).

Task 2 illustrates one aspect of our information-processing capacity.

TASK 2

Processing information

1 Look for about ten seconds at this line of numbers, cover them and see how many you can remember by writing them down:
1 0 1 0 0 1 0 0 1 1 0 1 0 0 1

2 How successful were you at remembering (processing the information)?

3 What strategy did you use to try to remember the information?
4 What helps us to remember and learn things by processing information?
5 Try this task with children. Discuss what helps them to remember.

Would practice on similar tasks improve children's ability to process this kind of information?

Think about the ways in which the mind can try to process into the memory such information. The mind tends to remember more when it can link units of meaning into patterns. A famous psychological study showed that the human mind can recall about seven (plus or minus two) unrelated items of knowledge.[4] Memory can of course be trained, for example, by making patterns out of the information given, and repeating these patterns until they become internalised as long-term memories. These patterns can be processed in different ways by the human brain. In what ways do you prefer to process information:

- verbally *through listening and saying or repeating the information*
- visually *through seeing visual patterns or pictures 'in the mind's eye'*
- logically *through seeing a pattern of logical or mathematical relations*
- physically *through physical representation or bodily gesture*
- musically *through melody, rhythm or musical association*
- personally *through linking information to personal experiences or memories*
- socially *through learning with and from others, sharing a task?*

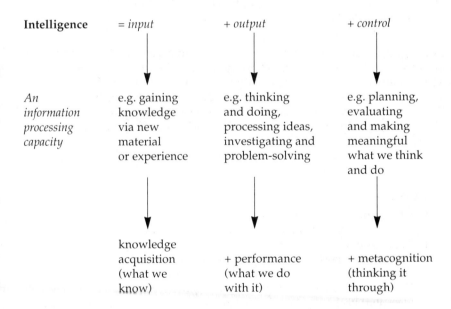

Intelligence	= input	+ output	+ control
An information processing capacity	e.g. gaining knowledge via new material or experience	e.g. thinking and doing, processing ideas, investigating and problem-solving	e.g. planning, evaluating and making meaningful what we think and do
	knowledge acquisition (what we know)	+ performance (what we do with it)	+ metacognition (thinking it through)

Figure 1.1 Intelligence as an information processing capacity

Humans are unique in their ability to process information through these different facets of their intelligence. Furthermore, human learning is most effective when it can bring these different 'frames of mind' into play. The seven different aspects of intelligence identified by Howard Gardner[5] and other researchers can be developed in the following ways.

Linguistic or verbal intelligence

We know from brain studies that specific areas of the brain are responsible for different aspects of language use. The link between language and thought has been the focus of much research and debate. Does thought, as Piaget taught, precede language, or, as Vygotsky argued, is language the vehicle for thought? Thinking involves the use of words and concepts, and cognitive development is closely linked to conceptual development. One way of helping children to develop their thinking is to help them to pattern or map out their concepts and ideas. Concept mapping (pages 57 ff) is one of a number of strategies that can help to enhance children's learning.

There are a various other ways in which the child's linguistic experience can be enriched, for example, by:

- reporting and explaining their news and views
- giving instructions on how to do things
- verbal argument
- doing or creating crosswords and word puzzles
- letter writing
- information finding, from newspapers, brochures, books etc.
- reading and writing poetry
- writing their own journals.

Creating their own journal or magazine can involve many aspects of language experience. Groups of children can contribute to one 'publication', or produce their own personal publications. At the age of ten, T. S. Eliot created a magazine called *Fireside*. In a three-day period during the Christmas holidays he produced eight issues. Each one included poems, adventure stories, news, gossip and humour. In his childhood efforts lay the seeds of future genius.

Why not try to create your own journal or magazine?

TASK 3

Creating a magazine
This can be a task for a child, or child and adult, or adults.
1 Create your own magazine.
2 Identify a purpose and audience for your publication.
3 Plan what it could include.
4 Think of a title, and how it will be put together.
Questions beginning, Who ...? What ...? Why ...? When ...? Where ...? How ...? may help with planning.
5 Use your linguistic intelligence – get publishing!

Visual/spatial intelligence

Evidence from brain research shows the left hemisphere is dominant in processing language, while the right hemisphere is crucial to visual and spatial processing. Visual/spatial intelligence is needed for all forms of problem-solving that require visualising objects and patterns. The making and understanding of maps is an example of the use of visual thinking. Activities that can help develop visual thinking include:

- map-reading and navigating journeys
- creating maps, e.g. of the neighbourhood or of imaginary worlds
- planning gardens, parks and recreation areas
- using diagrams and plans, e.g. in making models and construction toys
- designing routes or model layouts
- making a visual map of any given information, e.g. a recipe.

Goethe once said that we should talk less and draw more. Picasso completed 170 notebooks of sketches and experimental ideas which he regarded as essential raw material for his finished work. Drawing involves many thinking skills, as does the critical appraisal of works of art and design.[6] Other forms of spatial problem-solving include visualising objects 'in the mind's eye' (Can you see them from different angles?), and playing visual strategy games like draughts, chess and 'Othello'. Some of us are visual learners, or visiles, and learn best through visual means, but all aspects of learning can benefit from practice in visual thinking.

TASK 4
Visual thinking – draw from your 'mind's eye'!
Choose a picture that interests you, such as a magazine picture, photo or art print.
1 Study it carefully using your eyes and your mind.
2 Try to visualise the picture in your 'mind's eye'.
3 Then hide the picture and draw it from memory, trying to recall it as accurately as possible.
4 Compare your drawing with the original. How could it be improved?
5 How could you improve your visual thinking?

Logical-mathematical intelligence

Logical-mathematical intelligence is what is involved in scientific thinking. Along with language (verbal reasoning), it is what is usually measured in IQ tests. The development of this kind of intelligence has been carefully researched by Piaget and other psychologists. Brain research shows that some areas of the brain play a more prominent part in mathematical calculation than others. But the actual mechanism which accounts for some being brilliant at mathematics is not yet properly understood. We do know, however, the sorts of activities which will strengthen this kind of intelligence. These include the following:

- budgeting – keeping personal and family accounts
- planning journeys and outings
- practising mental mathematics, e.g. calculating amounts spent and change given
- calculating odds, chances and probabilities
- estimating quantities
- managing and planning time
- making timetables
- solving logical puzzles and problems.

One of the characteristics of logical-mathematical intelligence is the ability to see patterns and relations between things. The next task is an example of a way in which pattern-making can be encouraged.

TASK 5

Number patterns
1   Choose ten or twelve random numbers and write them down.
2   Study them and see what links you can find between any of the numbers.
3   What patterns can you make with them, e.g. by putting them in order, by making sums or sets from them – such as odds, evens, or primes?
4   What different patterns can you find?
    (For more mathematical activities, suitable for 7–12-year olds, see Fisher R. and Vince A., *Investigating Maths*, Books 1–4, published by Simon & Schuster.)

Physical intelligence

Control of movement is localised in the motor cortex of the brain, with each hemisphere controlling movement on the opposite side of the body. For example, right-handers control is usually in the left hemisphere. Many activities require physical intelligence to solve problems and achieve desired results. Carrying out a mime sequence or hitting a tennis ball may seem very different from solving a mathematical equation. Yet the ability to express emotion, as in dance; play a game, as in sport; or make a model, as in craft, design and technology, all involve physical problem-solving. This sort of 'hands on' experience, wanting to solve problems physically is, as in all intelligences, more strongly developed in some people than in others. But physical co-ordination has its corollary in mental co-ordination, and all physical tasks can benefit from a mindful approach.[7]

Some activities that can help develop physical intelligence, and physical problem-solving capacities are:

- developing knowledge and skill in a chosen sport
- craft activity, e.g. carpentry, clothes making and model making
- mastery of a physical discipline, e.g. dancing, martial art or gymnastics
- cookery, e.g. cake making and decorating

- 3-D puzzles, e.g. Rubik's cube, jigsaws
- machine maintenance, e.g. assembling, cleaning and maintaining mechanical appliances such as computer, bicycle or sewing machine.

The following task requires the application of physical intelligence.

TASK 6

Role playing
1 Choose a topic that you are currently reading, researching or learning about.
2 Think how to act, mime or role play some aspect of your learning experience, for example, mime a character from a reading book, television programme, historical period or foreign place.

Musical intelligence

Musical skill is another universal form of intelligence. Studies of human development suggest that all children have some 'raw' musical ability. This natural response to rhythm and melody may have its genesis in the rhythm of the mother's heartbeat and in the child's early attempts to understand the melodic pitch of speech sounds. Certain parts of the brain play important roles in the perception and production of music, largely in the right hemisphere. This intelligence can be highly developed in certain individuals. Yehudi Menuhin was smuggled in to hear orchestral concerts when he was three by his parents. The young boy was so entranced by the sound of the violin that he wanted one for his birthday – and a teacher. He got both, and by the time he was ten he was an international performer.

All children can be helped to develop their musical intelligence, and there is evidence that training in reading music can help development in reading and mathematics. The following activities can help stimulate musical intelligence:

- making music using a chosen instrument
- repeating songs heard clapping or beating time to music
- recognising and identifying tunes
- moving in time to music
- selecting appropriate music, e.g. background music to illustrate a story or poem.

TASK 7

Writing a song
1 Make up a song about something you are reading or learning.
2 Try writing a poem or rap and set it to your own music, or chosen musical melody and accompaniment.

Interpersonal intelligence

Interpersonal intelligence is the ability to understand others. As one child put it, 'I can't stand them, but I can *understand* them'. Piaget noted that one of the factors that limited the intelligence of young children was their egocentricity, namely the belief that the world revolves around them and their perceptions. Gradually the child begins to notice differences in others, in their moods, temperaments, motivations and intentions. Interpersonal intelligence develops from this basic capacity, and shows itself in the growth of social skills and with the ability to empathise with and learn from others.

Two key factors relate to the development of interpersonal intelligence in humans. One is the prolonged period of childhood, including close attachment to the mother. That the mother has a crucial role to play, in influencing the educational progress of children, has been borne out in many studies. The second factor is the importance for humans of social interaction. As Vygotsky remarked: 'We first learn with others what later we can do by ourselves.' All children benefit from opportunities of learning with others, in pairs and small groups, as well as by teaching others. Part of what they learn by working and playing with others are those interpersonal skills that make for success in life, including knowing how to co-operate with, learn from and lead others.

Opportunities to develop interpersonal skills include:

- listening to others through narratives, stories, poems, information and argument
- speaking to others as above, through teaching others, e.g. showing and telling
- helping others learn/solve problems
- caring for younger children or others who need help or attention
- co-operating in a team, discussing and contributing to a joint effort.

The following activity utilises aspects of interpersonal intelligence.

TASK 8

Making a presentation
1 Prepare a presentation to others which includes an explanation about what you are learning, e.g. a hobby or favourite pastime.
2 Show a visual element to illustrate your explanation.
3 Encourage the participation of others, e.g. by inviting questions or by including an activity.

Metacognitive intelligence

Metacognition (also called intrapersonal intelligence) is probably the most important aspect of human intelligence, for it is linked to the processing of all other forms of intelligence. It is the access we have to our own thoughts and emotions, to what we think and feel, and why we do things. It is at the heart of the Delphic injunction: 'Know thyself'.

From an early age, children have some understanding of the mind. By the age of three, they can use the terms 'know', 'think' and 'guess' to refer to mental states. By four, they understand what 'remember' and 'forget' means. By five, they are beginning to distinguish appearance and reality, and can answer the question: 'Is it real or not real?' After five, they develop metacognition through understanding more about the mind and brain, and the different elements of personality. They know more about what it is to understand something, what they believe and how beliefs can change. This growth of metacognitive knowledge is a key factor in the success of learning – in knowing how to plan, predict, remember, and find out.

These activities can help in developing metacognitive awareness:

- keeping a personal diary or journal
- planning how to use time
- predicting what you will be able to do well or have difficulty with
- discussing and understanding your feelings and moods
- recognising who you are like or unlike (see below)
- setting and achieving personal goals
- reviewing and evaluating what you have done.

The following task can encourage metacognitive reflection.

TASK 9

Thinking and writing – about me

Get some paper or your own book and a pen or pencil.

1 Think about yourself, or an area of your learning, and write under the following headings.

Who am I?

What I am good at?

What I am not good at?

What do I find interesting?

What do I want to achieve?

You might want to show this to others, or keep it to yourself!

2 If this description was read to your friends, without naming you, would they recognise you?

3 Ask your children to try this exercise.

What does research into learning tell us?

Research into learning is rather like the old story of the blind men and the elephant. Each feels one part of the animal and thinks it is the whole animal. The following represents some of the main research findings from the last 60 years.

Piaget

Piaget emphasised the view that thinking was an activity. We should allow children to have *thinking* time. This was highlighted for me when I was helping a group of children to build some model bridges. One girl sat in the corner doing nothing while the rest were busily engaged on drawing, talking and assembling their bridges. 'Come on,' I said, 'get busy.' The girl looked pained: 'Can't I have time to think?' she asked. I then realised that although she was sitting there she was also being active – thinking. The trouble with thinking is that you cannot see it, which is why teachers often look for evidence of 'business'. What Paiget said we should look for are signs of 'cognitive conflict'. To encourage children to higher levels of thinking we need to challenge their ideas, and offer what Yeats called 'the fascination of what's difficult'.

Bruner

Bruner's research emphasised the role of the teacher. It was not enough simply to let children think, work and play on their own. They need someone to 'scaffold' their learning, to lead them on to higher levels. One way of doing this is to help children to focus on the key concepts of what they are learning, and then revisit these concepts again and again. He likened this process to a spiral, coming back on itself, but at higher levels. The 'spiral curriculum' means that, if you wish to teach a child algebra at fourteen, you do best to begin at seven.

Vygotsky

The Russian psychologist, Vygotsky, found that social interaction was the key to success in learning. We learn more in collaboration with others – parents, other children and adults – than we can by ourselves. He rejected the view that intelligence was fixed. We all have what he called a 'zone of proximal development', referring to our potential for learning, given assistance by others. We never know for sure how far this boundary stretches. The role of the teacher is to try to realise this potential in students, and the main means of achieving that is through the use of language.

Linguistic theorists

Research by linguistic theorists has emphasised the value of talk in the development of thinking. We need to give children the opportunity to articulate their ideas, through talk and writing. In a sense we do not know what we think until we see what we say. The act of creating and communicating meaning forces us to think and re-think what we want to say, just as many teachers find that to get to know a subject really well you need to teach it. Or as one child put it: 'I didn't know I was going to say that until I said it!'

Curriculum research

Curriculum researchers have explored the way children construct their own theories. Gone is the view that children are blank slates to write on, or empty vessels to fill. From an early age they are trying to make sense of the world, and constructing their own theories about how it works and their own place in the scheme of things. Research in mathematics and in science shows that children draw their own conclusions and ideas from what they see and do. Sometimes their theories are strange and ill-founded. As a child, I was convinced that, if you took a bulb out of a light socket, the electricity would come flooding out. The trouble with wrong ideas is that they are very difficult to give up when they are your own. Even now my fears return whenever I am about to change a light bulb! Learning occurs when there is a change in what we think, and good teaching should be about helping children to construct and to re-construct their ideas.

Cognitive research

Cognitive research has focused attention on the complex nature of thinking. The mind has been likened to a community of intelligences. We have what Ornstein calls a 'multi-mind'. Researchers have found that we all have a different thinking and learning style. Some of us are 'audiles', who prefer to hear information, some are 'visiles', who prefer to see their information presented in visual form, and others are 'tactiles', who prefer concrete hands-on experience. Some prefer to work with others, with a partner or small group, and some prefer to work alone. The implication of these findings is that no one teaching style suits all students. What we need are a variety of strategies that can activate different facets of a child's intelligence.[8]

Psychologists

Psychological research has emphasised the key role of *self-esteem*, and our sense of mastery over what we think and do. We are better motivated when we think we are going to do well and when we are confident in our abilities, as in the old adage: 'Success comes in cans not can'ts'. We need to build a sense of 'can do' in our children. One way of doing this is by helping the child recognise their own achievements, increasing their awareness of themselves as learners. Another is to communicate to children your high, but realistic, expectations of what they can achieve (for more on self-esteem and mastery learning see Chapter 9).

Philosophers

Philosophy begins in wonder. Children share with the great philosophers a natural sense of wonder about the world. If they have around them people who can share in this wonder they are lucky indeed. Through the use of reason, they can translate their curiosity into ideas, theories and hypotheses about the way the world works. For the philosopher, Karl Popper, the prime characteristic of humans is that they are problem solvers, and of problems there is no end. Children will need to be problem seekers and problem solvers. For Popper, the form of human organisation best fitted to solve problems is the 'open society' – a community of enquiry in which all can share. The old schools of philosophy in Greece were places in which any topic or problem could be discussed, a useful model to offer the children we teach.

TASK 10

My theories of learning

Our ideas about learning come partly from our experience as learners and teachers, and partly from the example and ideas of others.

1 What has influenced you and your ideas about learning?
2 What are your theories about learning? Where do they come from?
3 Try to summarise your ideas about learning (in about 500 words), indicating what has influenced those ideas.

Summary

The thinking child is a learning child. From an early age, children can be introduced to complex ways of thinking, provided they are presented in simple and imaginative ways. Children are both 'at potential' and 'at risk' in their learning. If children are to realise their potential and avoid cognitive confusion, they need to develop thinking and learning skills. One way of helping them is to offer a specific thinking skills programme, another is to infuse thinking across the curriculum. Children pattern information in a variety of ways, and these different aspects of intelligence need to be developed through a thinking curriculum.

References

1 See Seymour Papert's (1980) *Mindstorms*, Basic Books, New York.
2 For a survey of research related to the CASE project as a programme of cognitive intervention and its effects on academic achievement see: Adey, P. and Shayer, M. (1994) *Really Raising Standards*, Routledge, London.
3 Bloom, B. and Krathwohl, D. R. (1956) *Taxonomy of Educational Objectives, Handbook 1: Cognitive Domain*, David McKay, New York.
4 Miller, G. A. (1956) 'The Magical Number Seven Plus or Minus Two: Some Limits on our Capacity for Processing Information', *Psychological Review*, vol. 63.
5 Howard Gardner's books include: (1983) *Frames of Mind: A Theory of Multiple Intelligence*; (1985) *The Mind's New Science: A History of the Cognitive Revolution*; (1988) *The Unschooled Mind*; (1982) *Art, Mind and Brain: A Cognitive Approach to Creativity*; and (1993) *Creating Minds*, Basic Books, New York.
6 Useful books linking art with thinking include:
Perkins, D. (1994) *The Intelligent Eye: Learning to Think by Looking at Art*, Getty Centre for Education in the Arts, Santa Rosa, Cal.;
Fisher, R. (1994) *Active Art: A Primary Art Course*, Simon & Schuster, Hemel Hempstead.
7 See Fisher, R. and Alldridge, D. (1994) *Active PE*, Books 1 and 2, Simon & Schuster, Hemel Hempstead.
8 For more on the cognitive aspects of education see: Fisher, R. (1990) *Teaching Children to Think*, Simon & Schuster, Hemel Hempstead.

2 Questioning

How questions can help develop thinking and learning

He that questioneth much shall learn much, and content much; but especially if he apply his questions to the skill of the person whom he asketh; for he shall give them occasion to please themselves in speaking and himself shall continually gather knowledge.
  Sir Francis Bacon (1561–1626)

It's harder asking questions than giving answers.
  Child, aged seven

When someone asked Isidor Rabi, a Nobel Prize winning nuclear physicist, how he became a physicist he told the story of his mother who, when he came home from school, did not ask the usual question: 'So what did you learn today?' Instead she asked: 'Izzy, did you ask a good question today?'

It is at home that a child first learns the power of asking questions. One research study found that four-year olds on average took part in 27 conversations per hour with their mothers, with each conversation averaging 16 turns.[1] Half of these conversations were initiated by the children who asked about 26 questions per hour. There was little distinction between working-class and middle-class families noted in the amount, frequency or content of talk. The researchers reported 'passages of intellectual search', episodes of persistent enquiry through conversation, in all types of family. At home, children are usually 'partners in dialogue' with their parents. What then happens to children when they go to school?

The study showed that when these children entered school their conversations fell to ten per hour with teachers, each lasting about eight turns. Teachers initiated most conversations and asked most questions. This, and other studies, show that, apart from speaking less at school than at home, children get fewer turns, ask fewer questions, make fewer requests for information, use less elaborated sentences, express a narrower range of meanings, and use language less often to plan, reflect, discuss or recall past events. There are fewer 'passages of intellectual search'. They are talked at, rather than talked with. This discontinuity between the culture of home and school can lead to educational 'disadvantage'. The ways in which teachers use language, and in particular use questions, can have immediate and long-term effects on children's learning.

Why do teachers ask questions? The common response is that teachers use questions in order to motivate, to test knowledge, and to promote reflection, analysis or enquiry. Questions are supposed to offer intellectual challenge, to encourage students to think. That is the theory. In practice many of the questions teachers use inhibit intellectual activity, and save students from the effort of having to think. Research, such as the Leeds Project,[2] shows that most questions teachers use are closed, factual questions with known right answers, making low levels of cognitive demand that do not encourage children to persist in their thinking and learning. An example of this occurred in a classroom when a teacher asked a six-year-old girl drawing a picture of a daffodil: 'What is this flower called?' The answer she received was: 'I think it's called Betty'.

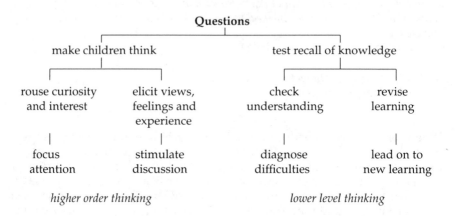

Figure 2.1 Some functions of questions

Teachers ask a lot of questions. Perhaps they ask too many questions. Researchers found that a group of teachers asked on average more than three hundred questions a day. The Oxford Pre-School Research Group,[3] which worked with nursery teachers and play-group leaders, found that adults who asked more questions were:

- less likely to receive questions from children
- less likely to promote elaborated answers from children
- less likely to encourage children to contribute spontaneously to dialogue.

The more the children were questioned the less initiative they showed in their responses. Most of the questions recorded in this study were of the closed variety, for example: 'What colour is it?', 'What is it called?', 'Where is it from?' Perhaps one of the lessons from this research is that we should try to ask fewer and better questions.

Asking the right question has been called the essence of teaching in the sense that it can provide a bridge between teaching and learning. Research into what makes schools effective places for learning identifies one common characteristic to be 'intellectually challenging teaching'.[4] One definition of a good question is that it provides an intellectual challenge. It stimulates what Piaget called the 'cognitive conflict' which may help children move on to a more advanced stage in their development. A good question can provide what Bruner calls the 'scaffolding' to new learning. A good question is like a candle in the dark, shedding light on both truth and mystery. But not all questions facilitate learning. What differentiates a good question from an unproductive one?

Unproductive questions

A poor question is a dead thing. It leaves thinking where it was and may limit, diminish or dismiss thinking. Some examples of unproductive questions are:

Stupid questions

These are questions that are thoughtless. They trivialise what is emotionally and intellectually complex. For example, a child whose mother had recently died was asked: 'How do you feel?' A stupid question will often provoke a thoughtless response. When the novelist T. H. White was asked by a doorstep evangelist whether he knew Jehovah, he replied: 'I am Jehovah!'

Too complex questions

These are questions too big or too abstract to be tackled at once. Once, hurrying along a busy street, I was accosted by a man with a clipboard who asked: 'Do you believe in God?' Somewhat taken aback, I replied: 'It depends what you mean by God.' As I moved on he said: 'I'll put you down as "Don't know".' A teacher began a lesson with the question: 'Why is there pollution?' There was no response from the class. It may have been more productive to have narrowed the focus, to have created a context, and to have moved from the known to the unknown.

Too closed, narrow questions

These are often the 'what-is-the-teacher-thinking?' type of question. When too easy, they can result in the phenomenon of the hit-and-run barrage – 'What is this ...?, 'What is that...?', 'What is the other ...?' When too hard they can result in the teacher-answered question. A teacher once asked her class: 'What is a frog?' Getting no answer she progressively answered the question herself: 'An — a — am — amph — amphib — amphibian!'

A major obstacle to thinking is the search for the 'quick-fix' of a single correct answer, the game of 'guessing what is in the teacher's mind'. An example of this is taken from the Leeds Project research:

Teacher	What day was it yesterday?
Child 1	Tuesday.
Teacher	Was it?
Child 2	Thursday.
Teacher	What day is it today?
Child 2	Wednesday.
Teacher	Today is .... What day is today?
Child 1	Wednesday.
Teacher	What have we just had this morning? [No response.] What did we have this morning when we came to school?

Pupils   Wednesday! Thursday!

There is a place for the quick, closed, fact-finding question of the quiz-type. A memory test can reinforce and remind pupils what they know, and can help them to remember. We all enjoy showing off what we know – when we know the right answer. For specific purposes, like mental arithmetic, low-level closed questions can provide a significant cognitive challenge. The acid test of a question is: Does it provide a worthwhile challenge? In providing challenge, there needs to be a balance between the closed 'quick-fix' questions, and open questions that demand more complex and higher order thinking.

Higher and lower levels of thinking

Bloom's taxonomy can be set out as follows.

Higher order

- *Evaluation*, e.g. 'What do you think about … criteria to assess or judge…?'
- *Synthesis*, e.g. 'How could we add to … improve, design or solve …?'
- *Analysis*, e.g. 'What is the evidence for … parts or features of …?'

Lower order

- *Application*, e.g. 'What other examples are there …?'
- *Comprehension*, e.g. 'What do we mean by …? Explain …'
- *Knowledge*, e.g. 'Who … What … Where … When … How …?'

According to Bloom's taxonomy of thinking skills, *evaluation*, *synthesis* and *analysis* demand more complex and 'higher' levels of thinking. Questions which ask for *application, comprehension* and *knowledge* demand less complex and thus 'lower' levels of thinking. One effective questioning strategy is to ask questions that make increasing cognitive demands on students, to move from simple knowledge/recall questions, through questions that ask for comprehension/explanation, and application, then analysis, synthesis and evaluation. Often this will mean moving from the 'What' and 'How' descriptive question, to the 'Why' and 'What for?' question that asks for a more complex response. A good question fits into a pattern that offers progressive and productive challenge to learning. It offers a model for the sorts of productive question that students can ask of themselves and of others.

Good questions

Research shows that many teachers fall into the trap of asking too many questions – too many closed and low-level questions. We shall get a better learning response from children if we act as follows.

- Ask fewer, but better, questions *Two or three thoughtful questions are better than ten that we have not thought about. Aim for quality, rather than quantity.*
- Seek better answers *With fewer questions, we have time to invite more*

responses, and to extend thinking time. Withhold the rush to judgement. Work at getting a better response.

- Encourage children to ask more questions *The ability to question is one of the keys to effective learning, and it comes with practice. Value children's questions as much as their answers.*

One of the characteristics of a good question is that it avoids the trap of a 'yes' or 'no' response. When one teacher was getting her children to evaluate their work she asked: 'Are you pleased with the way it's worked out?' Later, after listening to a tape of the discussion, she realised her questions required only a 'yes' or 'no' response. Whereas, 'How well do you think it has turned out?' would have invited more.

Examples of open-ended questions, that genuinely invite children to think, include the following.

- What do you think?
- How do you know?
- Why do you think that?
- Do you have a reason? How can you be sure?
- Is this always so?
- Is there another way/reason/idea?
- What if ...? What if not ...?
- Where is there another example of this?
- What do you think happens next?

A good question makes the mind buzz. It offers a challenge to thinking; a search for understanding. They are troublesome, rarely rooted in certainty, and invite an open-ended, thoughtful response. They are productive for they generate something new. Examples of such questions could include:

- judging *Is it ever right to steal/tell a lie/kill someone?*
- comparing *In what ways are these two objects/pictures/texts/actions similar? In what ways are they different?*
- evaluating *Which is the better picture/text/object/action ...? Why?*

The best questions provide both challenge and interest. Consider the topic of birds. What questions might arouse students' interest and be a challenge to their thinking? Consider some alternatives.

- What is a bird?
- What do you know about birds?
- How is a bird like a cat?
- If you were born again would you want to be a bird?

TASK 11

Devising good questions

Think of a topic of interest.

1 Devise the most *challenging* questions you can about the topic that are suitable for your chosen audience. Select those which you think are the most *interesting* of these questions.

    2   Ask others (your students in groups) to devise questions about your topic.
    3   Discuss which are the best questions, and why.

A teacher of a class of thirteen-year olds was due to give a lesson in science on gravity. She thought a useful way to start would be to find out what the pupils already knew about the concept. So, to begin the lesson, she wrote on the board the following questions.

- You drop a ball from your hand. It falls. Why?
- You are standing on the surface of the moon. You drop a ball. What happens? Why?

The class were divided into small groups to discuss their ideas about each of the questions, and to record their conclusions. The questions stimulated a variety of explanations, many expressing assumptions in unscientific terms. In response to the first question, one group stated: 'The ball falls because of the air'. Answers that mentioned the key word, 'gravity', provided no insight into the level of real understanding. In response to the second question, another group wrote: 'The ball drops very slowly because the gravity on the moon is much less than on earth'.

    The collection of this information took 20 minutes, and the pupils enjoyed the exercise. It was the first time the teacher had used such a questioning strategy, and later commented she 'was amazed by the range of ideas that the pupils came up with'. The act of writing down responses to the questions is a way of making explicit the initial ideas of the students, and provides a reference point against which any development of ideas can be judged. When we are given answers to our questions – whether in written or verbal form – how should we respond?

Thinking time

'What is truth?' said jesting Pilate and would not stay for an answer. When you have asked a question, how long do you wait for an answer? A good answer is worth waiting for. The composer Stravinsky once advised musicians: 'Value your intervals like dollars'. Also, in questioning, we should learn to value silence. Research has shown that some teachers, on average, wait only one second for an answer. If an answer is not forthcoming within a second, teachers tend to interject by repeating or rephrasing the question, asking another question, or another child. When a pupil answers, teachers tend to respond within one second, either with praise, or by asking another question, or with a comment. Rarely, it seems, are students allowed the luxury of a thoughtful silence. We want to keep the conversational ball rolling, but studies show that by increasing thinking time, also called 'wait time', the quality of pupils' responses can be dramatically increased.

    How long should we allow for thinking time? Increasing 'wait time' to three seconds can result in significant changes, such as:

- pupils giving longer answers
- more pupils offering to answer

- pupils willing to ask more questions
- pupils' responses becoming more thoughtful and creative.

Strangely, teachers find it very difficult to sustain a longer waiting time. Old habits die hard and the 'scatter-gun' approach of quick-fire questions and answers soon reappears. It is not only pupils who need time to think. There are two elements of thinking time – after the question and after the answer. The two elements are:

- thinking time 1 *the teacher allows three seconds to encourage longer, more thoughtful answers from pupils*
- thinking time 2 *the teacher models a thinking response, values complexity and defers judgement.*

Allowing silence is, then, a deliberate act by the teacher to encourage a more thoughtful response, as in this example below.

Teacher	What makes a good piece of writing?
Child 1	When you write neatly.
Teacher	Hmm [pauses].
Child 1	Like it's a good story — and it's easy to read.
Teacher	Ahh — easy to read. What else ?
Child 2	Well it has to have a good beginning or you don't want to carry on — I mean it's got to be — exciting — make you want to go on reading it.

Questions that can help us focus on the ways we use talking for thinking include the following.

- Who is doing the talking and the thinking?
- Am I allowing enough thinking time (thinking time 1 and 2)?
- Do I support students in their talking and thinking? How?

There are various ways in which pupils can be helped to participate and to make their own meanings. What fuels their response? Different students need differing sorts of stimulus. Often the 'puzzled listener' role will be effective, if it reflects genuine interest and attention to the student's answer. Strategies to support thinking and talking include pause, prompt and praise.

Pausing

Pausing means giving time, thinking time, and opportunities for re-thinking and re-stating an idea. 'Can you explain/Tell us again …?'

Prompting and probing

Prompting and probing gives verbal encouragement, for example, by 'reflecting back' to check whether we have understood what the student has said. Following the pupil's train of thought and encouraging deeper exploration is sometimes called 'probing'.

Examples of probing questions include:

- Why do you think that …? How do you know …?

- Can you tell me more about ...? Can you show me what you mean?
- What if ...? Is it possible that ...?

Sometimes a minimal encouragement will prompt further response – 'Hmm', 'Umm', 'Uh huh', 'Yes?', 'OK', 'I see', 'And'.

Non-verbal reinforcement includes eye contact (the eyes are the windows of the soul), facial signals, e.g. smiles, body gestures, (e.g. nodding on rather than nodding off!), and other signals of approval.

Praising

Praise gives positive feedback and is specific and personal. Responses such as: 'That's an interesting answer Jan', 'Thanks for that answer Pat', can foster general participation by:

- supporting the hesitant
- rewarding the risk-takers
- valuing every genuine contribution.

One way of valuing and encouraging contributions is to put all ideas and suggestions on display, perhaps with the child's name next to each contribution as a focus for further discussion, writing or research. The skilful use of questioning can help turn the classroom into a 'community of enquiry' in which all are involved.

Questioning skills

Kerry[5] has identified seven questioning skills. These are:

- pitching the language and content level appropriately for the class
- distributing questions around the class (to the shy as well as the 'stars')
- prompting and giving clues where necessary
- using pupil's responses (even incorrect ones) in a positive way
- timing questions and pauses between questions
- making progressively greater cognitive demands through sequences of higher-order questions
- using written questions effectively.

There is a danger, even with skilful questioning, of following a pre-set agenda, and not encouraging student initiative. In adopting a 'teacherly role' we can dominate the talk by asking too many questions and imposing our own meaning. One way to avoid excessive teacher control is to actively encourage pupil-to-pupil exchanges. Ways to do this include:

- withholding judgement *responding in a non-evaluative fashion, asking others to respond*
- cueing alternative responses *'There is no one right answer. What are the alternatives? Who has a different point of view?'*
- inviting student questions *'Anyone like to ask Pat a question about what she/he has said/done?'*
- allowing for students questioning each other *'Ali, would you ask someone*

else what they think/what their ideas are?'
- using 'think-pair-share' *allowing thinking time, discussing with a partner, then sharing with the group.*

Those teachers who ask too many questions tend to discourage students from giving elaborate or thoughtful answers. Those who force on pupils a pattern of repetitive questions – who?, what?, where?, when?, why? – will face pupils who ask fewer questions themselves, give short responses, rarely discuss with peers, volunteer few ideas and show many confusions. What then is to be done? One answer is to use alternatives to questions.

Alternatives to questions

Teachers (including parents and any care-givers) who model thoughtfulness will encourage their children to exhibit more thoughtful behaviour. Teachers who offer their own thoughts and ideas, who speculate, suggest, and hypothesise, will create an environment in which speculation, hypothesis and argument can flourish. As a teacher I would regularly talk to myself, 'thinking aloud', and through this gained not only a useful reputation for eccentricity but also found my pupils more willing to think and talk things through for themselves.

The questions I would ask, as 'think alouds', to model self-regulation of the thinking process might include the following.

- What am I going to do/write/say now?
- What is my problem? What sort of problem is this? Where have I seen this before?
- What am I doing now? What do I need to do? What can I try?
- Who can help me? What do I need? What is the next step?
- How am I doing? How will I do it? How have I done ?
- Is there a better way? What alternatives are there? What must I remember?

One researcher wrote: 'Higher order thinking involves imposing meaning, finding structure in apparent disorder.'[6] Or as one child put it: 'Thinking is talking it through with yourself when you have a problem.'

The following are kinds of 'talking it through' statements that can encourage a more thoughtful response:

- a speculative statement *'Perhaps …' – playing 'devil's advocate' to stimulate response*
- a reflective statement *'You seem to be saying that …' – to encourage elaboration*
- a state-of-mind statement *'I don't quite understand …' – to invite further response*
- a request for information *'I'd like to hear what you think about ' – to extend discussion*
- an invitation to think *'I want you to think carefully about this …' – to cue a more thoughtful response, or to invite a question.*

Encouraging children to question

If we want pupils to be active and adventurous thinkers we need to encourage them to ask questions. As children become older this becomes less easy. Researchers[7] found that those children who were asking over 50 per cent of questions at home, were asking under 5 per cent of the questions once they got into school. So how can we encourage pupils to be more active in questioning and seeking after knowledge? Two ways of trying to establish a climate of enquiry are for teachers to:

- model a questioning mind by thinking aloud and asking good questions
- value and provide opportunities for students to ask questions.

When a class of ten-year olds was starting the study of a country the children were put into groups to brainstorm questions on: What do we want to know about our country? The groups were then to share, display and discuss their questions which were to act as stimulus-points for the research project.

In a class of younger children someone had brought in a snail. The teacher could have used the snail simply as an opportunity for 'look and say', but after the usual knowledge/understanding questions: 'Where was it found?', 'What do you know about snails?', 'Where can you find out about snails?', she encouraged the children to ask their own questions. They soon came up with the usual sorts of questions: 'Can they hear?', 'What do they eat?', 'How do they move?' but the one they found most interesting was: 'Do snails love each other?' There was a lively discussion about possible ways to find answers to this question!

If children, themselves, identify what they want to know by asking a question, then they are much more likely to value and remember the answer. Some questions will not be easy to answer. One teacher, when asking children if they had any questions about current news, was asked: 'What is the difference between the ozone layer and the greenhouse effect?' She did not feel able to give a full answer at the time so she gathered a variety of responses from the children, displayed the question in the classroom, involved them in researching an answer and even got in a 'expert' to judge the different answers to the question.

This brings us to another characteristic of questions – like good wine, questions can improve with keeping. Display them, savour them and come back to them. Find some more. Sort them into categories, for example, question that we can answer, questions that we can find the answer for and questions that cannot be answered.

Discuss with the children the nature of questions. Give them a list of questions and ask them which they think is the best or most interesting question. Discuss good and bad questions. Find out what questions they would like to have answered.

Can the students think of any questions that can never be answered?

Create a poem about questions, for example like that in Figure 2.2. on the opposite page.[8]

What is the mystery
　　　　　　of the funny
　　　　　　　　　question mark?
　　　　　　　　　　　How
　　　　　　　　　　　　does
　　　　　　　　　　　　　it
　　　　　　　　　　　　　　happen?
　　　　　　　　　　　　　Did
　　　　　　　　　　　　　　someone
　　　　　　　　　　　　　　　twist
　　　　　　　　　　　　　　the
　　　　　　　　　　　　　　long
　　　　　　　　　　　　exclamation mark
　　　　　　　　　　so
　　　　　　　　　it
　　　　　　　　had
　　　　　　a head?
That's how they
found out
a new
meaning
to
this thing.

Do you
under-
stand?

Figure 2.2 Poem by Karen, aged ten: *What is the mystery of the funny question mark?*

TASK 12

Generating questions

Chose a topic, working in groups of two or three. The teacher also brain-storms/devises back-up questions.

1 Share and analyse the questions together.
2 How many questions can you create?
3 What are the most interesting questions?

Another way of encouraging a self-questioning approach is to have a Think Book or Learning Log in which children can write about what they feel and think, and be invited to answer that key question in all learning: 'What does this mean to me?'

Assessing the ability to question

A simple way to assess the ability of children to devise questions is to give them a common object such as a chair or cup and ask them to list as many questions about the object as they can. Another way is to take a subject of current study and see how many questions children can create about the topic. A third way is to choose a text, such as a part of a story or poem and see how good they are at interrogating the text, by asking them to create questions about it. With practice at creating questions from a variety of source materials, the fluency and flexibility of their questioning will improve. After a year in an enquiring classroom, children will often be able to generate twice as many questions, under test conditions, as they were able to create at the beginning of the year.

Test your questioning power by choosing an everyday object and seeing how many questions you can create about that object. How many questions do you think it is possible to generate? (The answer is not known, for the possibilities are theoretically limitless.)

Given practice in asking questions, they will be able to see more, to think more and learn more about any object or aspect of life – and should with experience improve the quality and quantity of their questioning.

The following are some of the kinds of questions that children can create after looking at an object.

Looking at an object – some questions that can be asked

1 Physical features

What is it?
What is it called?
What does it look like?
What colours/shapes/textures does it have?
What does is it feel/smell/sound like?
What is it made of?
Is it made of natural or manufactured materials?
Is it complete?
Has it been altered, adapted or mended?

2 Construction

How was it made?
Who made it?
Was it made by hand or machine?

3 Function

What was it made for?
How could it be used?

4 Age

Is it old?
How old is it?

5 Value

Is it valuable?
What is it worth?

6 Origin

Where does it come from?
Where was it made?

7 Design

Is it well designed?
How is it decorated?
How could it be improved?

Creating a questioning classroom

There can be problems in creating an enquiring classroom. The questions of children can be challenging and unsettling. It will not suit the teacher who thinks they have all the answers. It will not suit the teacher who is afraid of being intellectually challenged. It will suit the teacher who is keen to help children to be independent, creative and curious. It will also help to keep alive children's own curiosity about the world, and about themselves. In an enquiring classroom I was once asked: 'Mr Fisher, what are you going to do when you grow up?' In another I thought I would offer a philosophical challenge to some nine-year olds. I said: 'How do you know that I am Mr Fisher?' After a silence, one child replied thoughtfully: 'How do you know *you* are Mr Fisher?'

However these questions are answered, perhaps there is a clue to creating an enquiring classroom in the mnemonic – PARTS ARE EQUAL – reportedly used in the human awareness training of traffic wardens, meaning: *People Always Respond to Someone Actively Encouraging Equality in Questioning and Listening*

Some examples of classroom activities which are designed to create questions for thinking are set out on the following page.

Study questions

Help students identify what is significant in their learning. Groups should devise questions from their study, writing or textbook, to test themselves or others.

Reading review questions

Ask your pupils to help you ask the class questions about the story they are reading or listening to. Try to get the child to identify what kind of question it is, e.g. is the question asking for information that is 'on the lines' (explicit), 'between the lines' (implicit), or 'beyond the lines' of the story?

Hotseating

A student chooses to be a character from literature, history or current affairs. The others brainstorm questions to ask the child-in-role. Encourage open questions.

Twenty questions

One or more of the students chooses either an object, person or place. The others have 20 questions with which to find out the answer. Only 'Yes' or 'No' answers are allowed. Only three direct guesses are allowed. Play in groups of six students. Two select the topic and four ask the questions.

Question and answer

Students devise questions to fit a given answer, for example, for younger students a person, place, thing or number; older students can devise questions for a quotation from poem or play.

Blockbusters

Create a board of letters (as in the television game). The students devise questions for each letter on given theme. The teams, in turn, aim to answer or complete a line of letter questions across the board, and block opponents.

Any questions?

Students ask or write down any question (real, hypothetical, factual or metaphysical). Each question is then given to an 'expert' partner to answer.

Interview questions

Decide on someone to interview, for example, a visitor, or a local VIP. The students then devise, share with each other, evaluate and prioritise the best interview questions.

Question your classroom

Devise, write and display questions to stimulate thinking and discussion about objects, pictures or texts of interest in your classroom.

Keep a questions box, board or book

Collect any interesting or puzzling questions that arise in the classroom. Create a place to write, store or display your questions, such as in a box, on a board or in a book. Set aside some time, such as at the end of the week, to choose and discuss a question. Alternatively share out the questions for children to work on at home or swap questions with another class or group.

TASK 13

Creating a questioning classroom
Some questions for reflection or discussion include the following.
1 Do teachers ask too many questions ?
2 What can be done to shift from closed questions to those which genuinely invite the children to reflect and solve problems?
3 How can teachers encourage children to ask questions?
4 What should be done about children's questions?
5 How do you create a questioning classroom?

Summary

Questioning lies at the heart of teaching and learning. There is some evidence that teachers ask too many closed and unproductive questions. We should aim to ask fewer but better questions, and seek from our students better answers, giving them time to think and to respond. Teachers help children learn by being discriminating in their use of questions, and by encouraging students to ask their own questions. All children should have opportunities to generate questions and their ability to do so will improve with practice. We should aim to create enquiring classrooms – where children's questions are valued, and where genuine learning and understanding are promoted.[9]

References

1   Tizard, B. and Hughes, M. (1984) *Young Children Learning*, Fontana, London.
2   Alexander, P. (1992) *Policy and Practice in Primary Education*, Routledge, London.
3   For more on the Oxford Pre-School Research see: Wood H. and Wood D. (1983) 'Questioning and the Pre-School Child', *Educational Review*, vol. 35, no. 2.
4   Mortimore, P. et al. (1988) *School Matters*, Open Books, Wells.
5   Kerry, T. (1982) *Effective Questioning*, Macmillan, London.
6   Resnick, L. (1987) *Education and Learning to Think*, National Academy Press, Washington D.C.
7   Tizard, B. and Hughes, M., op. cit.
8   Reprinted by permission from Fenwick, G. 'Young Gifted Children Writing Poetry', in Jones, L. (ed) (1993) *Curriculum for Able Children*, NACE/NAGC University of Middlesex, London.
9   For more on research into questioning see:
    Morgan, N. and Saxton, J. (1991) *Teaching Questioning and Learning*, Routledge, London;
    Wragg, E. R. (1993) *Questioning*, Routledge, London.

3 Planning

Learning to plan is an essential skill for learning how to learn

A mighty maze! but not without a plan.
  Alexander Pope (*An Essay on Man*)

I've got a plan, it's quite complicated and may not work, but at least it's a plan.
  Child, aged nine

Learning to learn is about learning to think, and, in particular, about thinking ahead. But children often do not realise the importance of thinking ahead and do not get systematic instruction in planning. They learn how to perform tasks and procedures, but not how to use planning skills in all areas of the curriculum. The links in learning between subjects are not always made clear, nor are the connections between classroom learning and the informal world of learning that happens outside of school. If there are general planning and problem-solving procedures that apply equally to the classroom and the real world then children need help in learning them. But are there general planning and problem-solving skills and, if so, what are they?

One way to investigate whether there are general problem-solving skills is to look at the way expert problem-solvers work. What factors make for successful performance in varying fields of human endeavour? When looking at expert performance in diverse fields such as mathematics, athletics, art, novel writing, science or cookery one common factor is that experts spend more time in planning and preparing for their activity than novices. Problem-solving in any area of human endeavour is complex and makes considerable demands on cognitive skill and processes of premeditation. Whether it is for cookery or calculus some essentially similar mental processes are used. Where outcomes are successful there have been efforts, to plan the process, to adapt and refine the operation of the activity, and to keep performance under review.

Experts have much more knowledge in their domain than novices. They also have cognitive skills that allow them to deal with problems, and enable them to turn thoughts into successful action. Many of the problems that we, and experts, face each day have common elements.[1] Every problem-solving situation requires a decision – even a decision to make no decision – a plan of action, a set of actions, and a way in which to tell if our goal has been achieved. Are these skills general or are they particular to every situation?

There is some debate about whether there are any problem-solving skills of a general nature that can be applied to a number of different tasks. One view is that problem-solving means having specific knowledge relevant to a particular situation. Many subject teachers in secondary schools subscribe to the view that the special skills and knowledge that they teach are subject-specific and non-transferable. However, others argue that there are a number of general competencies that are involved in all problem-solving activities regardless of the subject or specific situation. These general skills relate, in particular, to planning, monitoring and evaluating, what has been called the cycle of 'plan-do-review'.[2]

Planning for problem-solving

In some cases students will need specific instruction in what strategy to employ. At other times awareness of more general problem-solving processes may be all that is needed to tackle a specific task. Typically, direct instruction is needed for novice learners and those with learning difficulties. For students who are older and have well established basic skills, more general problem-solving procedures may be more appropriate. These general problem-solving processes can be summed up in the following series of steps:

- defining the problem *What do we want to achieve?*
- gathering information *What do we need to know to tackle the problem?*
- forming a strategy *How can we tackle the problem?*
- implementing the strategy *How are we tackling the problem?*
- monitoring outcomes *Have we achieved our aim?*

Successful problem-solving involves the systematic application of a sequence of thoughts and activities, in other words, planning. A plan is a set of steps or sequences that we believe will lead to success in a task. A plan does not need to be a set order of steps. Often plans need to be flexible to allow for the use of a range of possible strategies that may help in achieving our objective. As we move to a solution we may need to try out new ideas, to take account of new obstacles and changing circumstances. Planning in its simplest form means we have thought about what we are going to do. 'Chance favours the prepared mind', said Pasteur. In teaching children how to plan we are teaching them to be thoughtful about what they are doing, to be best prepared to achieve success in learning.

Some researchers regard planning as the most important of cognitive methods that we can use in the classroom.[3] Planning helps students to deal with information in any subject in an organised and systematic way. Planning can be regarded as the key working process of the brain in its higher functions, and fundamental to the success of human learning.[4] Even very young children can begin to link actions together to achieve goals. Planning is evident in the way children solve construction problems with building blocks, persuade parents to let them watch an extra hour of television or unfasten child-proof locks. Young children do not recognise that they are creating plans, and they cannot explain the planning process to others. However, they do come to understand the distinction between mental activity such as wanting things, and actions such as eating food.[5] They are able to manipulate in their minds simple mental constructs and

ideas of physical things to achieve certain goals. It is a functional understanding. They do not consciously recognise that certain actions are necessary to achieve a goal. It is only later that they come to understand what
they are doing, and why. They become aware of the concept of a plan, that
certain actions can be linked together in a conscious and premeditated fashion. Plans begin to become 'blueprints for thinking'.[6]

Young children learn how to perform tasks, before they are able to
understand what they are doing and why. This development of understanding has implications for educators. Children need help in gaining
insight into ways of performing tasks successfully. They need help in
understanding and in making use of various levels of planning. These
levels of planning can be summarised as:

- unconscious planning
- specific planning
- strategic planning.

Unconscious planning

In unconscious planning the person performs the task without being aware
of a plan, or, the need for a plan. Problem-solving is then a matter of doing
rather than design. To the question: 'Why are you doing that?' The child
might reply: 'I don't know, I just do it and it comes right'. Certain kinaesthetic tasks such as riding a bike, or building a tower with blocks may not
require conscious planning. The danger is that some children apply this
level of undifferentiated planning to all learning tasks, regarding success in
problem-solving as something to do with good fortune or coincidence
rather than design – 'you either can do it or you can't'.

Specific planning

Specific planning involves a conscious effort to develop a plan for a specific
task. The individual is aware of the goal and can articulate some steps in
helping to achieve the goal. For example, a child makes a plan of a story
before writing it, or an adult plans the lay-out of a new garden. There is a
systematic attempt to reach a goal, but there may not be awareness of other
strategies or approaches to the problem. In particular, a specific plan may
founder on an unexpected obstacle. A problem arises and the plan does not
seem to work. There may not be an answer to the question: 'What will you
do if you get stuck?' or 'What happens if it does not work?' if the planning
is too narrowly specific.

Strategic planning

Strategic planning is deliberate planning activity which includes consideration of potential obstacles and the need for flexibility in the use of strategies. An approach to a task may include a number of alternative routes.
Planning is flexible to include changes in the sequence as circumstances and
conditions allow. Examples might include the tactics devised by a sports
team to cope with varying conditions of play, or the way children might
plan to create a magazine together to take account of different contributions

in the group. To be effective strategic planning needs a conditional element, reflected in the question: 'What would happen if....' It recognises the need for alternative plans of action if events or circumstances change.

'The best laid schemes o' mice an' men, Gang aft a-gley'. Why? One reason is that the various elements of the planning process need to come under metacognitive control.

Planning and metacognition

Metacognitive control is one of the characteristics of good thinking and learning. Students with good metacognitive control, those we might call 'meta students', have control over their thinking, they think ahead and are mindful of consequences. They are aware of strategies that can help them in their thinking, such as the need to concentrate, and knowing what to try when you get stuck. They think about their own thinking, and become efficient in using these strategies. But many students do not have insight into their own thinking and learning. Those with poor metacognitive control, 'non-meta students,' are mentally passive and unreflective. They believe that learning is externally controlled. They are not aware of strategies that might help them to think better and learn more efficiently. They are inefficient in the use of strategies, for example, by being impulsive in their responses and having an episodic grasp of reality that often characterises poor learners.

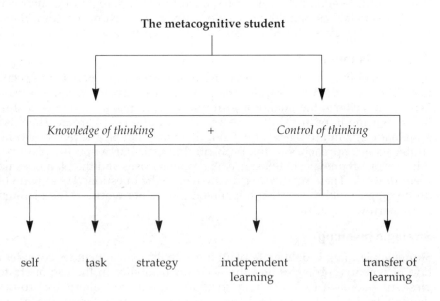

Figure 3.1 The metacognitive student

Metacognition has three major elements:

- planning *planning goals (and sub-goals), operations and sequences, identifying obstacles and possible problems, knowing the process and predicting outcomes*
- monitoring *keeping in mind the goals, place in the sequence, possible obstacles and errors, knowing what to do when things go wrong or plans fail, knowing when goal is achieved*
- assessing *assessing success of strategies and progress towards goal achievement, assessing errors and mistakes along the way, evaluating the whole process.*

Piaget spoke about the importance of the 'groping and correcting' phase of learning, which is why the monitoring and assessing elements of metacognition are so important. Planning needs to be flexible and strategic to take account of the unexpected. History is littered with examples of rigid plans that failed, such as Napoleon's march on Moscow in 1812. A specific plan may focus too narrowly on one goal and fail to take account of changes in circumstances. Planning also needs to be personal, to be rooted in what we know and understand, and attuned to our styles of learning and doing.

Children need to be made aware of planning, to be shown examples of plans and to be given the opportunity to create their own plans. If our aim is to develop independent learners, we need to try to move from teacher-controlled plans to student-controlled planning. This can be achieved in three phases:

- direct instruction phase *explaining to students about plans and planning, showing examples of plans and planning strategies involving students in recording or implementing given plans*
- facilitation phase *explaining how plans can be created, showing how plans can be modified and extended, involving students in putting plans into their own words*
- self-generation phase *explaining that everyone needs to be able to plan, showing examples of students' planning, involving students in making their own plans.*

If planning is essential to success in problem-solving and for developing metacognitive skills, then children should have the opportunity to learn about the process of planning and be given experience in planning for specific and strategic purposes. The school curriculum provides the ideal context for introducing the planning process to children. So what contexts can be used for teaching planning?

Teaching planning

Using examples from everyday life is the best way to illustrate what planning is, and to bridge the gap between unconscious and conscious mindful planning. One approach is to introduce children from an early age to real life problems and tasks that require planning.

I became aware of one approach to teaching about planning during my first year of teaching. One of the problems I faced was what to do first thing on a Monday morning, or at any time when there was nothing timetabled. At breaktime, I would ask children from other classes what their teachers did. I soon learnt that one young teacher had the problem solved. Every Monday morning she would sit her class down and tell them at least one of the problems she had faced at the weekend, or had to face in the previous week. (Needless to say, she did not, I think, share all her problems.) But her children were fascinated, firstly, to find out she was human and had problems and, secondly, that these could be shared and talked about. How could she buy something she wanted but could not afford? How should she tile the bathroom? How should she get to know her new neighbours to whom she had never spoken? Whether these problems were real or imaginary I never discovered, but I knew from the way children would come up to me in the playground and whisper confidentially: 'Do you know what problem she has this week?', that she had found a powerful motivator of interest, and a useful tool for discussing alternative plans of action.

TASK 14

Planning for problem-solving
1 Identify a real-life problem from your own experience.
2 Share this problem with a child or group of children, expressing the problem at the child's level of understanding.
3 Ask the child to suggest a plan by which the problem could be solved.
4 Some questions to consider include the following.
   What is the action plan? What steps are needed?
   What are the logistics of the plan? What resources will be needed?
   What are the criteria for success of the plan? How will we know if the plan has worked?

If one resource for discussion is to talk about plans to overcome problems in the real world, another is the use of favourite stories. Many stories that we share with children have a planning element which can be found in the theme or plot. The following are some questions that could be asked of young children about almost any story that they read or hear.

- What problem(s) did the hero/heroine face?
- What was his/her plan to solve the problem in the story?
- Did the plan work? Why?

An extension of this is to ask children what they would think and do if they were the character in the story. For example, what plan could they think of if they were one of the three pigs trying to stop the wolf from destroying their house and eating them? Many stories contain a turning point, when a dilemma is faced and a decision is made. These are good moments to pause, and to encourage some thinking time. For example, in the story of Sleeping Beauty, when the king and queen know that the princess is under a curse which means that if she pricks her finger she may sleep for a hundred years, what should be their plan? Should they warn their daughter? Is she better off knowing or not knowing about the curse? What should they do?

Another obvious way of introducing the need for planning is the daily programme. What should we do? When should we do it? When should we stop? Why should we do it this way? The child's timetable of activities at school and at home provides good opportunities to discuss the need for forward planning. Research in schools shows that many children do not know what they are going to do in class later that day or later that week. Many have no clear idea of the pattern of their daily activities. The following are some possible timetabling activities for children to plan:

- daily plan *record/discuss their planned timetable for the day*
- weekly plan *record/discuss the planned timetable for the week*
- long-term plan *record/discuss the major events of the term or year*
- weekend plan *record and discuss how they plan to spend the weekend (or an ideal weekend)*
- study plan *record a timetable for study, e.g. homework, or study plan for a project*
- holiday plan *record and discuss their holiday or vacation plan*
- life plan *record and discuss their possible future life plans.*

Planning can begin at an early age. The High Scope[7] pre-school/nursery programme for three to five-year olds has a planning element built in to daily activities. The day begins with the children sitting in a group and each saying what their plan for the morning is, what activities they intend to undertake and in which order. Planning behaviour is reinforced by the expectation that they will collect the apparatus they need from marked storage areas and return the apparatus to the appropriate place. The children are expected to review at the end of the session what they did and how their plan worked. Some young children find planning various activities throughout a morning quite a challenge. Others learn how to plan for the day, for a week and even longer. They learn that through planning they can bring order, structure and predictability to their world, even if it is just in the prepared environment of the classroom. They are no longer passive recipients of information about what to do, but can be active in planning purposeful activities. If one of the purposes of school is to practice the things you need for life, then practice in planning at any age must be a useful aim of teaching and learning.

TASK 15

Creating a time plan

1 Identify a period of time to plan, e.g. a day, week, month, term or year.
2 Show children how activities can be created, e.g. on a timetable. What would be the timetable for their class in an ideal school?
3 Ask children to:
   Identify a purpose for their time plan
   record their planned activities for the chosen period of time
   present and discuss their finished plans.

Children do not need to plan every activity. Part of learning to plan is to know when planning would be helpful. Opportunities to plan exist in, and can enrich, every area of the curriculum.

Any sequence of activities that make up a lesson is a plan, and can be introduced by saying: 'The plan for this lesson is ...'. A plan should not merely be a set of directions or instructions which tell children to perform one action after another. A plan should include some reference to the process of thinking and learning. The planning process should include some reference to thinking about, monitoring or assessing the outcome of the task.

Figure 3.2 illustrates a plan for learning how to spell a word. It shows an example of a child making the plan his own, after discussion with the teacher, and adding his own drawings.

Characteristics of well-formulated plans

There are a number of features characteristic of well-formulated plans. The unconscious, undifferentiated plans used in everyday life may only include a goal and some general idea how to achieve it. They are rarely written down, seldom contain specific details of how to proceed and are not open for others to follow. A well-formulated plan provides a framework which enables people to think through future actions. It helps us to organise and structure understanding and assists us in undertaking practical tasks. A good plan, such as the one illustrated in Figure 3.2, contains a number of important features:

- focusing *Where to start? How to start? 'Look.'*
- acting *What to do? In what sequence? 'Cover.' 'Write.'*
- monitoring *Is the plan working? What do we need to remember? 'Think.'*
- evaluating *Is the task completed? Has the plan worked? 'Check.'*

It is important that plans provide a starting point. A clear beginning or *focus* shows a student where and how to start and what to do, and what steps or *actions* to take. The aim of the plan is to liberate the student from direct teacher assistance. Plans are not only a teaching device, but aim to provide a means for independent learning. A good plan contains an action component and a thinking component. Good plans need *monitoring*, which means providing thinking (metacognitive) steps to help people in making judgements about what they are doing and intend to do. Without the monitoring and *evaluation* stages, a plan can remain just a set of directions for a given task. A good plan is strategic, and includes skills that can be applied in a number of contexts.

A strategic plan should encompass the FAME formula (focus, act, monitor and evaluate), but may not necessarily have only these four steps. Some plans may include many more steps, such as two focusing, three acting and so on. In some plans, a step may have a dual function, for example, acting and monitoring, or monitoring and evaluation may be just a single step. Having too many steps becomes confusing. A useful task is for the teacher to do a model plan in great detail, and ask children to try to simplify the steps in their own words. Keep in mind the magic number seven (plus or

Figure 3.2 A child's plan illustrating 'Look, Cover, Think, Write, Check'

minus two) as the ideal number of steps in a finished plan.

Once children gain understanding of the planning processes, and have used them for a number of purposes they will become more proficient and confident in planning. They will be able to draw on knowledge of past planning experience to guide them in future planning. As children become more independent learners and problem-solvers, they will develop planning skills in the following four areas:

- knowledge of what plans are, and experience in using plans
- skill in formulating plans for different purposes
- understanding when planning would or would not be useful and appropriate
- the disposition to plan and to be mindful (strategic) in undertaking tasks and solving problems.

Planning works best when it meets student needs. One need that everyone faces in school is the need to communicate through writing. All writing requires planning, or some form of mental rehearsal. Planning can be important in the pre-writing stage.

Ways of using plans

Plans can be used in a variety of ways: before attempting a task, during the task or after a task is completed. Plans can be created individually, in pairs, small groups or as a whole class. Plans can serve a variety of purposes:

- a plan to help you …
- a plan to help your group …
- a plan to help others …
- a plan to show how you did it …
- a plan to show others how to do it ….

All areas of teaching provide opportunities for planning. The following is a list of some of the possible opportunities for planning in different subject areas:

- language *plans for activities in reading, writing, speaking and listening*
- mathematics *plans for solving problems, to show methods and procedures*
- science *plans of investigations and experiments*
- technology *plans for designing and making*
- history *historical plans, battle plans, plans for historical research*
- geography *plans for field trips, plans for geographical research*
- art *plans for art projects*
- music *plans for performing, composing or appreciating music*
- physical education *plans for gymnastics, dance and sports sequences*
- religious education *plans of religious festivals, rituals, customs etc.*

All research, whether it is carried out by an industrial or university research team, or research undertaken by children at home or school, can benefit from planning. A useful first step in any research activity can be to ask some key questions. The following task contains a number of questions to help in planning research.

TASK 16
Planning for research
On a chosen topic list, or ask students to make lists, under the headings set
  out below.
1   What do we know about the topic?
2   What do we need to know?
3   How can we find out? Where? Who might help us?

Many practical activities around the school can provide opportunities for
planning and problem-solving, for example, preparing for a class outing, a
class presentation, party or fund-raising activity. Older students can be
asked to plan their homework schedules, and to provide plans for important elements of course work. Children can be encouraged to talk about
their own plans, such as plans for family holidays, plans for winning
games, or plans on how to make friends.

A plan for painting a picture

The following is an example of a child's plan for painting a picture.

1   Look at the subject you are going to paint. Think about the dimensions,
    sizes and colours of each part. Take into view the distances and shapes
    and weigh them up in your head.
2   Roughly sketch the scene in charcoal or dark pencil. Check your sketch
    and compare it with the scene. Make sure you are happy with each line,
    for this is the skeleton of your picture.
3   Look carefully at your colours and prepare the paints in your palette.
    Use just the right amount of paint for the style of your painting.
4   Now start blocking in the basic colours. Slowly, but surely, work your
    way round the picture adding details, and remembering to do the back-
    ground first. After a while, it is a good idea to stand back from your
    painting and view your work so far.
5   By now, you should have covered the whole sheet with paint and can
    begin on the details. If you are painting a landscape, think about adding
    a few birds or, if a seascape, a few boats. Maybe, you could even add a
    couple of people – just use your imagination. If you are painting a por-
    trait or a still life picture you could perhaps add highlights or shadows.
6   When you have finished your picture, stand back and look at it to make
    sure everything is to your satisfaction.

Planning does not ensure success, but it does increase the likelihood of success. At the very least it encourages 'mindfulness'.[8] Planning is a fundamental skill for learning and for life and should be part of the daily experience of
all children, as it is of all teachers. 'Plans help me to think things through,'
said a nine-year old. Have you made or shared any good plans today?

Summary

Planning is a key process for effective learning and problem-solving.
Children need help in making use of different types and levels of planning.

The ability to plan, particularly strategic planning, helps the metacognitive control of learning. Important aspects of the planning process involve monitoring and evaluation. If planning is important, it should be part of the daily experience of children, infusing all areas of the curriculum. The teaching of planning should be structured so that it moves from teacher-generated planning to students being more effective in making their own plans. Planning can play a part in all curriculum areas and is an important lesson for learning and for life.

References

1   Bransford, J. et al. (1986) 'Teaching Thinking and Problem-Solving', *American Psychologist*, vol. 41, pp. 1078–89.
2   Fisher, R. (ed.) (1987) *Problem-solving in Primary School*, Blackwell/Simon & Schuster, Hemel Hempstead.
3   Ashman, A. and Conway, R. (1993) *Using Cognitive Methods in the Classroom*, Routledge, London.
4   Luria, A. R. (1973) *The Working Brain*, Penguin, Harmondsworth, and (1980) *Higher Cortical Functions in Man* (2nd edn), Basic Books, New York.
5   Wellman, H. M. (1990) *The Child's Theory of Mind*, MIT Press, Cambridge, Mass.
6   Friedman, S. I., Scholnik, E. K. and Cocking, R. R. (eds) (1990) *Blueprints for Thinking: The Role of Planning in Cognitive Development*. Cambridge University Press, Cambridge.
7   Hohmann, M., Banet, B. and Weikart, D. P. (1979) *Young Children in Action: A Manual for Pre-School Educators*, High Scope Education Research Foundation, Ypsilanti, Michigan.
8   Langer, E. (1989) *Mindfulness*, Addison-Wesley, New York.

4 Discussing

Talking to learn through dialogue and discussion

As civilised human beings, we are the inheritors, neither of an enquiry about our-selves and the world, nor of an accumulating body of information, but of a conver-sation, begun in the primeval forests and extended and made articulate in the course of centuries. It is a conversation which goes on both in public and within each of ourselves .... And it is this conversation which, in the end, gives place and character to every human activity and utterance.
   Michael Oakeshott

You don't know what you know until you say it.
   James, aged nine

James is a quiet boy. In a class of lively nine-year olds, he can be easily overlooked. As a rather isolated and undemonstrative child, his abilities could easily be underestimated. In a group, he strives to be invisible. But sometimes, as in this lesson, his conversation flowers. It was a discussion in a Philosophy for Children class (see page 52), talking about whether the brain is the same as the mind. 'You know a lot of things', said James, 'but you don't know what you know until you say it.' His argument seemed to be that there were many things, items of knowledge and such-like, stored in the brain that you only knew about if you brought them to mind. Sometimes this 'bringing to mind' occurs in dreams, sometimes in thoughts and sometimes in speaking. Much of our knowledge is tacit. Once articulated, this knowledge no longer simply resides in tacit form. When articulated, it is no longer what Whitehead called 'inert knowledge'. When it becomes available for inspection, it is available for performing a variety of tasks. This 'bringing to mind' through talk can be a powerful thinking and learning strategy. It is part of the long tradition of Socratic teaching, which begins from a seeming ignorance and proceeds through dialogue to a revealed understanding. The Socratic quest of philosophical enquiry, through questioning and self-questioning, can be seen as a method for getting at personal meanings that may otherwise remain hidden. Socrates, like James, believed that we know more than we know. We may only be dimly aware of the nexus of meanings within which we operate. We may not know what we think until we hear what we say. This perhaps underlies the Delphic injunction 'Know thyself', a process that is served by thought and talk.
   This chapter considers some of the links between talk and thought, from the egocentric talk of the young child, through the many different forms of dialogue, to various ways of talking to learn through discussion in a classroom community of enquiry.

Talk and thought

There has been much debate among philosophers and psychologists into the relationship between thought and language. Does thinking determine language, or does language determine thought? Or is there an interactive relationship between the two? Verbal thinking can be regarded as the internalisation of speech. The structure of our thinking in a typical conscious thought does not, however, seem to mirror the patterns of fully voiced speech. Vygotsky[1] argues that a better approximation to verbal thought lies in egocentric speech. When children, or adults, talk to themselves about what they are planning or doing their egocentric speech captures something of the function of thinking. Consider the following from Joyce's *Ulysses*:[2]

> ...*that lovely fresh plaice I bought I think I'll get a bit of fish tomorrow or today is it Friday yes I will with some blancmange with black currant jam like long ago not those 2lb pots of mixed plum and apple from the London and Newcastle Williams and Woods goes twice as far only for the bones I hate those eels cod yes I'll get a nice piece of cod* ....

and compare it with the following from a five-year old:

> *I'm going to make a now what do I want. Let's see.... I'll start with this and fix it on ... like this. Is it right? It's got to go up ... wait and see. Brrrrrm! It needs some more ... not that one. OK what's next? It's got to look right ....'*

As with thinking, egocentric speech has a self-directed regulative function in which the child seeks to represent and respond to the world. As Vygotsky says:[3]

> ···*the function of egocentric speech is similar to that of inner speech: it does not merely accompany the child's activity; it serves mental orientation, conscious understanding; it helps in overcoming difficulties; it is speech for oneself, intimately and usefully connected with a child's thinking.*

From an early age, children are busily engaged in creating meaning out of what William James called 'the great buzzing, blooming confusion of the world'. They begin to develop 'theories' about what they know and experience. These ideas become the basis of their actions and responses and are tested, validated, revised or improved in the light of subsequent experience. They help the child to anticipate, comprehend events, and to create order out of what would otherwise seem to be random and inexplicable. If this meaning-making capacity is adequate, and subject to testing against reality, then they can achieve competence in their lives. The relationship between the inner world of mind and the outside world becomes creative. Our competence in solving a mathematical problem, painting a picture, or maintaining a personal relationship all depend on this capacity to construct meanings, from the interaction of ourselves and our environment. Inadequate meanings lead to inadequate responses, to poor levels of anticipation and an inability to comprehend the consequences of ideas and actions. Socrates summed this point up succinctly when he said: 'The unexamined life is not worth living'.

TASK 17

Talking and thinking – a discussion plan
Discuss with some children the relationship between talking and thinking.
The following questions can be used in discussion.
1   When you talk do you always think first what you are going to say?
2   Can you talk to someone without thinking?
3   Do you ever talk without thinking?
4   Which comes first thinking or talking?
5   Is thinking just talking to yourself?
6   Can you think without words?
7   Can you talk without words?
8   Which can you do more quickly talking or thinking?
9   Do you ever talk to yourself? Why?
10 Does talking with others help you think and learn? Sometimes? Always?
Never? Why?

Modelling – recreating the world in words

One way of helping this construction of understanding is to talk with ourselves about our experiences, to model the world as we understand it in
words. Vocalisation gives substance to thinking. More accurately this is sub-
vocalisation, for the words do not need to be audible. As adults, this 'talking
things through' to oneself may seem a natural enough activity. We do not
have to see Shakespeare's *Hamlet* to know the experience of a 'stream of con-
sciousness' soliloquy. For children, at the early stages of self-awareness, it is
an experience to be encouraged. Teachers can encourage this process by modelling it themselves, by talking things through out loud or as a soliloquy.

Examples of talking things through

Define the problem
Say what the situation is, where you are and where you hope to get to and
ask questions like: What is the situation? What do I want to achieve? What
obstacles prevent me from doing it?

Plan a course of action
Talk through a step-by-step approach to a problem, outlining what one
hopes to achieve and the stages one hopes to go through. We know from
research that a key factor that differentiates experts from novices in most
fields of activity is that experts spend more time at the planning stage. Part
of the skill of planning is predicting the consequences of an action.
Questions in the planning process include: Where do I start? How do I
start? What do I need to do? What will happen if I do this?

Monitoring the situation
Check the progress of a plan, action or experience by asking, for example:

How am I doing? Is it working as expected? What needs doing/thinking about? What should happen next?

Reviewing the outcome

Verify that the task has been achieved by testing the result by asking: Is it finished? Does it make sense? Have I achieved what I set out to do?

Self-questioning

In sports coaching, much stress has been placed on the value of the 'inner game', on the belief that planning, anticipating and framing models of play in our head will help improve subsequent performance. Developing the inner game through self-conversation is just one way to do it. As one child reported: 'I like talking things through to myself – no-one interrupts!' It helps the child not only in 'coming to know', but also in their knowledge of themselves – the skills of metacognition.[4]

All successful learners have metacognitive skills that involve developing an awareness of their own learning. If children are made aware of their own learning then they are in a better position to improve it. By modelling examples of talking things through we can show children ways in which they too can articulate their ideas. We learn to find out more by questioning ourselves, and talking through what we have done, what we are doing and what we hope to do. This self-questioning is in a sense the first stage of Socratic dialogue. If we are to invite children into the club of critical thinkers we need to share with them our own thinking processes, and also invite them to share in the thoughts of others – through dialogue.

Thought and dialogue

Wittgenstein[5] argued that the limits of one's language are the limits of one's world, and, as far as our verbal intelligence is concerned, he is surely right. 'Whereof one cannot speak,' he wrote, 'thereon one must remain silent.'[6] As the work of Luria and Yudovich[7] shows, in their classic study of identical twins, creating a social context where dialogue takes place and where children are persuaded to make their meanings public, and therefore explicit, produces gains in thinking and learning. From an early age, the boy twins had developed a private language of their own (a restricted form of Russian), that could not be understood by their teacher or classmates, when, at the age of five years, they went to school. Their play and social understanding was as limited as their speech. The less backward twin was put in an ordinary class and, after six months, his language had improved to the average level expected of the class. The more backward twin was given, in addition, a carefully mediated programme during which he was forced to articulate his meaning and understanding. This boy made even more spectacular progress, out-performing his brother in both verbal and non-verbal intelligence tests.

Children need opportunities not only to enquire into their own views and ways of thinking, but also, through dialogue with others, to discover different perspectives and points of view. It is through dialogue (as well as through other symbolic means, such as the written word, art, dance, music etc.), that the private world of the self is extended, and we are able to overcome the egocentricity of thought by being helped to find more reflective and considered ways of thinking. Through dialogue, inner speech is turned into a shared event – what Harri-Augstein[8] has called a 'learning conversation' and what others have referred to as 'conferencing'.[9]

A learning conversation can be structured round any event or experience. What differentiates a learning conversation, or conference, from ordinary talk – from day-to-day chat and routine conversation – is that it involves higher-order thinking and raises the process of learning into awareness. A learning conversation contributes to understanding. It involves helping children to express their understanding about what they are doing. A learning conversation, therefore, involves some form of positive cognitive intervention. It does not leave everything as it is. It challenges and it invites response. The teacher becomes, in a Socratic sense, a 'gadfly', challenging the status quo of students' thinking by asking them to express their personal understanding of the topic in hand.

Some examples of strategies teachers can use to encourage students to articulate their thinking through dialogue, and encourage them to become participants in a process of enquiry are:

- defining the purpose of the activity, by discussion *Why are you doing this? What do you hope to achieve? How will it help (e.g. to fulfil your needs/ambitions, or the needs of others)?*
- inviting views or opinions about the topic in hand, by asking questions *What do you think? What are your views/opinions/beliefs about the topic? Do you agree with what has been said?*
- questioning the text or topic, to encourage self-monitoring of understanding *What do you not know or understand about it? What do you want to find out? What questions can you ask about it?*
- clarifying to help students express what they mean by asking questions *What does that word/point/detail mean? Can you explain it? Are you saying that…?*
- summarising, to check understanding of the whole of the topic *What was said? Can you say it in a few/your own words? Can you say what you think/know?*
- developing strategies and tactics, by discussion *How can you succeed/do well? What problems/obstacles do you face? What ways can you try (to succeed/overcome problems)?*
- evaluating outcomes, by discussion *Have you succeeded? What is good about what you have done? What could be improved?*
- reviewing the whole process, by discussion *Would you do this again? Would you do it this way? What have you learnt from doing it?*

Any learning activity consists of a number of sub-events out of which the whole experience develops. There is, therefore, a double-focus to any activity or dialogue, the parts (separate instances, events, experiences, actions, ideas etc.) and the experience or topic as a whole. Dialogue needs to focus, therefore, on both general principles and particular examples. It needs to provide insight into parts (analysis), and an overview of the whole (synthesis). One of the advantages of group discussion is that it offers the possibility of including a variety of viewpoints, of exploring the particular individual views of students, as well as the general or organising principles that help to make sense of the topic as a whole. Discussion provides an opportunity to learn what others think, and to express and clarify our own thinking. Discussion can be a powerful vehicle for learning – but what is it, and how should we use it in the classroom?

What is discussion?

The word discussion has two common uses. The first is as a general term to cover a wide range of informal situations where talk between people occurs. According to one researcher there are more than a dozen forms of discussion, including debate, panel forum, buzz groups and peer tutoring.[10] The second use has a more specific meaning. This refers to a particular form of group interaction where members join together to address a question of common concern, exchanging different points of view in an attempt to reach a better understanding of the issue. This form of discussion has also been called a 'community of enquiry'[11] and it is this 'ancient and essential educative activity'[12] of interpretative or enquiry discussion which will be explored.

Certain conditions can be identified as necessary for a discussion to take place. These include a subject or topic to be discussed, people to discuss it, and certain language or behaviour to facilitate the discussion. If the discussion is to be a genuine process of enquiry it should reflect certain defining conditions, moral dispositions and intellectual principles. 'The central function of discussion is the improvement of knowledge, understanding and/or judgement .... Discussion differs from the social art of conversation in that what the talk is about is a matter of some serious importance.'[13]

Defining conditions

Certain characteristics or logical conditions define discussion. These are the conditions that have to be met for us to say that people are actually engaged in discussion. They include that people participating in a discussion:

- must talk to one another
- must listen to one another
- must respond to what others say
- must put forward more than one point of view on the topic under discussion
- must intend to develop their knowledge, understanding or judgement on the issue.

The following questions can be used to assess whether a genuine discussion has actually taken place.

- Have children talked to one another?
- Have they listened to each other?
- Have they responded to what others have said?
- Have they considered different viewpoints?
- Have they shown development of knowledge, understanding or judgement?

These conditions define what discussion is, but they are matters of degree. All discussion must involve some form of interaction but, in the classroom, these conditions can be seen to develop and improve over time, for example, by students talking more, listening more attentively, responding more to what others say, putting forward more divergent points of view and being able to correct and refine their judgements.

Moral dispositions

Certain moral principles underlie the successful working of group discussion. Without a moral framework, group discussion cannot function. The moral principles that make discussion possible include:

- orderliness *by observing the rules of discussion such as 'only one speaks at a time', not interrupting or shouting someone down*
- reasonableness *whereby individuals are willing to listen to the reasons, evidence and arguments of others, and are willing to allow the arguments of others to influence their views*
- truthfulness *speaking what they believe to be true, not deliberately lying, deceiving others or pretending to believe what they do not believe*
- freedom of expression *being free to express an opinion, not subject to restraint by the views of others, by being ridiculed or embarrassed*
- equality of opportunity *with all having equal access to opportunities to speak and to have the attention of others, not having to suffer the dominance of the few*
- respect for others *respect for the rights and opinions of others, giving attention and thought to what they say, responding with care and respect for them as persons*
- open-mindedness *being open to the views of others, willing to change one's mind, being sensitive to the views of others, and willing to suspend judgement.*

If classroom discussion always reflects moral principles and dispositions such as these, then it will help to foster the intellectual qualities or virtues of participants. If students and teachers take care to exhibit these attitudes and concerns during the course of discussion, they will grow in these qualities and become a model for others. The cultivation of understanding will be enhanced by being responsive to the opinions of others, by being reason-seeking in argument, reflective in judgement, and by communicating in a clear, concise and consistent fashion. These intellectual virtues play a vital role in the search for meaning and order in a confusing world. They help strengthen the ability to make reasonable judgements about what to think and do.[14]

TASK 18

Why use discussion?
What are your views on the use of discussion?
The following questions about the use of discussion could help frame your own thinking, or can be starting points for discussion with colleagues or students.
1 What is a discussion?
2 Is every kind of talking together a discussion?
3 Do discussions need rules? If so, what should they be?
4 What good can come out of discussing things with others?
5 What do you like/not like about discussions?
6 Can you remember a good discussion? (What made it good?)
7 What things are best for discussion?
8 Are there some things you would not want to discuss?
9 Do you prefer to talk or listen in a discussion?
10 What would you like to discuss?

Teaching through discussion

There has been much research in recent years into the ways in which teachers generate talk with and between children. Much of this impetus in the United Kingdom has come from the National Oracy Project,[15] involving hundreds of teachers and advisers. Close attention has been given to the use of talk in the classroom, often involving the analysing of evidence on tape. This has highlighted the value of exploratory talk, of talking round, talking through and talking about topics of study, as well as the importance of having a purpose and an audience for talk. Talk needs to be directed to an end, towards a question, or focus of enquiry or as part of a learning conversation. Talk for its own sake may be congenial, but it is often unproductive, as the idle chatter of children in unsupervised groups often shows. But the tapes and observations of teachers also revealed ways in which teachers sometimes negated their purpose of supporting learning through talking.

Teachers confirmed what much research into classroom interaction had suggested, that in their conversations teachers took up more talking time than children. The recommended interviewer/interviewee ratio of talk should be about 20 : 80, but teachers often find that they themselves do not provide good models for discussion. 'I heard myself dominating the discussion', said one teacher, 'interrupting children, asking questions and rephrasing answers, and, worst of all, not listening to what they said.'[16]

In classroom discussion, children tend to talk directly to the teacher, competing for attention, or become monosyllabic in their responses. They become dominated by the need for approval, rather than by the search for understanding. They tend to be fearful of taking risks, inhibited from exploring the unfamiliar, or from building on the ideas of others – all aspects of talk that need to be developed if children are fully to explore their ideas. This is partly due to the standard forms of classroom discourse, where the teacher takes on the role as the provider of answers and the dispenser of approval. Such established patterns are hard to alter, but in building a genuine community of enquiry, there is a need to make explicit any changes that are being made in the 'educational ground rules'.[17]

The ground rules for 'talking to learn' should include the teacher making clear their role in the learning situation.

The teacher as expert

There are many situations where teachers need to take on the role of expert, sustaining the attention of individuals or groups, leading pupils to higher levels of understanding through direct teaching methods. This means 'scaffolding' the steps to learning and understanding so that students achieve their optimum potential in assisted learning or performance. This may be achieved, for example, by explaining, by questioning or by demonstration.

The teacher as facilitator

Teachers often organise situations where children are working in groups. In this role the teacher has a management function rather than a direct teaching role. The children may be free to explore ideas and to help each other in a collaborative venture without constant reference to the teacher, although the teacher may intervene when pupils do not seem to be getting on. Students can benefit from working collaboratively without teacher intervention, and can become skilled at managing group interactions, for example, ensuring that each member of the group has a turn. It is helpful if groups have had a chance to establish and agree the ground rules for discussion beforehand.

The teacher as participant

Discussion between pupils can often be useful, but talk for learning is generally enhanced by the active participation of a teacher or experienced adult. The benefits that a teacher can bring to an enquiry or learning conversation include the following elements of mediation:[18]

- focusing *by directing attention to important points, issues or factors*
- seeking meaning *by asking for reasons, explanation or clarification*
- expanding *by showing links between ideas, and links to new ideas*
- rewarding *by verbal or non-verbal expressions of positive response.*

One of the purposes of a teacher as participant is to get pupils to talk and listen to each other, rather than directing all their talk through the teacher. The aim is to help children to feel independent and equal in their responses to each other, and to create what Lipman calls 'a community of enquiry'. Some strategies that have helped in this process include:

- the teacher sitting at the same level as the children, as one of the audience
- everyone sitting in a circle and being given a turn to speak if they wish
- using a symbol, e.g. a 'talking shell' or 'magic microphone', where only the person holding the object can speak
- encouraging speakers to look at the person to whom they are talking
- think-pair-share, where each child has a 'talk partner' so that together they can think, discuss and contribute.

- asking a child to chair a group discussion
- listening more than you speak, allowing 'thinking time', using eye-contact and supportive interjections, like 'Mmm' or 'Yes...' to encourage children to expand on their meaning
- giving your own opinion, idea or experience to stimulate thought instead of asking too many questions – sometimes playing 'devil's advocate' by arguing an opposite viewpoint.

When can talking to learn can be stimulated in the classroom?

TASK 19

Contexts for discussion
What are the possible contexts for encouraging discussion in the classroom?
1 Make a list of possible opportunities within the curriculum where talk may help thinking, understanding and learning.
2 Consider your contexts under three headings.
   a) Teacher as expert
   b) Teacher as facilitator
   c) Teacher as participant.

Research suggests that 11-year-old children are more competent at telling a story than they are at argument and non-narrative forms of writing or discussion.[19]

All areas of the curriculum can provide opportunities for learning conversations and enquiry – or specially devised thinking skills programmes can be used for this purpose. Philosophy for Children[20] is one such programme. Below is a brief summary of the processes involved, followed by an example of a discussion using the Philosophy for Children approach. The format for a philosophy for children lesson involves:[21]

- children reading part of a philosophical story round the group or class
- after reading the story, children are asked what they found interesting or curious, and to choose an idea they would like to discuss
- children's responses are written on a board in the form of questions, with their name written alongside their question
- a question is chosen from the board to form the basis of enquiry and discussion.

The following dialogue is an excerpt from a Philosophy for Children session, and was prompted by reading part of *Harry Stottlemeier's Discovery* by Matthew Lipman.[22] The comments come from a group of 11-year-old children. After raising several questions from the reading, one was chosen for discussion.

RF   Is your brain the same as your mind? Let's see if we can get a bit closer to an understanding of that. Tom, why did you ask that question?

Tom	Well is it — I mean your brain controls your heart and your arms and everything that goes on in your body, but does your mind really think, 'Okay — I'll move left,' and do you think, 'OK brain send messages down to the muscles to move?'
RF	So are you saying because the brain has its messages that the mind is not aware of that, it means that the mind cannot be the same as the brain?
Tom	Yes, it isn't the same as the brain, — because — it's part of the brain but it isn't the brain.
	[This age-old question in philosophy prompted a number of comments from children, agreeing, disagreeing, suggesting or building on ideas.]
Child	I think I'd agree with Tom that your mind is part of the brain. But — if you'd like to put one inside the other you'd put the mind inside the brain
RF	So if the mind is inside the brain....
Tom	Or inside part of it ...
RF	Part of it. How do you think it's different from the brain? If it's not the same as the brain — it must be different, mustn't it?
Tom	Well the brain controls everything about us, the mind as well, but the mind only controls our thoughts — and contains our thoughts.
Child	Memory?
Tom	I think the mind is made out of memories and thoughts — it's a thinking bank.
RF	So is the mind the same as the brain, but the brain just bigger than the mind, or is the mind different from brain?
Child	Different?
Child	Yes.
Child	Because it doesn't control anything — the mind just thinks.
Child	The mind, I think, is our thoughts more than controlling our body. I mean — our brain sends messages everywhere round our body all the time to nerves and everything, or they are sending messages to the brain but the mind isn't part of this, I don't think. I think the mind just contains your thoughts.
Child	And memories.
	[The discussion moved on to what happens when you die.]
Child	I think when your brain dies it's like a shut down, and it shuts down your body. And I don't think your mind does carry on really, it just shuts down every system, and your brain has to work your mind really, because I don't think your mind would really work if your brain had shut down.
	[The children went on to discuss what happens in the mind when you dream, and were then encouraged to think of analogies for the mind.]
RF	Would you agree with someone who says the mind is a bit like smoke in the brain — a sort of strange ghost?
Child	Yeah.

Child	Yes.
RF	If it's like a strange ghost, then could it live outside the brain?
Child	Not like a ghost.
Child	The mind's not like that — it's not very good.
RF	Not a good way to describe the mind? A lot of thinking goes on in what are called analogies. We've got to liken it to something else to understand it better. What would you say the mind is like?
Child	Like a big warehouse — with things on the back shelves of your memory — and things being moved around in your thoughts.
Child	Yeah.
RF	So part of the warehouse is called the mind? The active part …?
Tom	No, the warehouse is your mind.
	[Discussion continued on how the mind was like a warehouse.]
RF	If the mind is like a warehouse what is the brain like? Can you continue this analogy …?
Child	A brain is like a — a — beehive.
Child	A dock — containing lots of different warehouses for doing different things.
Child	An ants nest!
	[The topic ended with children being offered a 'last word', and the chance to sum up their thoughts.]
RF	So if we come back to Tom's question, 'Is your mind the same as the brain?', we could now formulate a much better answer to that couldn't we?
Tom	Yes.
RF	How would you sum up your answer now, Tom?
Tom	Your brain is like a dock and your mind is like a warehouse in it containing all your memories and thoughts on lots of different shelves — and your brain sends out different messages around and across the dock.

Socrates was called a 'midwife of ideas', and this is an apt description of any teacher who seeks to develop talk for learning. Talking to learn can be considered to be an aspect of cognitive apprenticeship. Key elements in this process include:

- modelling *demonstrating self-questioning and the articulation of ideas*
- coaching *encouraging the articulation and questioning of ideas through dialogue*
- practice *providing opportunities for talking and learning in a community of enquiry.*

Talking to learn, as the above transcript shows, is not an exact art. It is a process of learning to think and reason through learning to talk with, and listen to, others. The teacher models the process 'teaching by example' and mediates the process, both by building on what children can contribute and by providing opportunities for enquiry to take place. This exemplary role of the teacher is summed up well in the words of Michael Oakeshott. 'Not the cry, but the rising of the wild duck impels the flock to follow it in flight'.[23]

Summary

Talking and thinking are closely linked in the child's attempts to reflect on and make meaning out of experience. Aspects of talking to learn include talking things through to oneself, dialogue with others, and group discussion. The teacher can help children to develop communicative competence through discussing matters that require the exercise of thought and judgement. Curriculum activities and thinking skills programmes, such as Philosophy for Children, can provide contexts for discussion and enquiry.

References

1   Vygotsky, L. S. (1962) *Thought and Language*, MIT Press, Cambridge, Mass.
2   Joyce, J. (1968) *Ulysses*, Penguin, Harmondsworth, p. 685.
3   Vygotsky, L. S., op. cit. p. 133.
4   Ibid.
5   Wittgenstein, L. (1961) *Tractatus Logico-Philosophicus*, Routledge & Kegan Paul, London.
6   Wittgenstein, L. (1922) *Tractatus Logico-Philosophicus*, 7.
7   Luria, A. R. and Yudovich, F. A. (1971) *Speech and the Development of Mental Processes in the Child*, Penguin, Harmondsworth.
8   Harri-Augstein, S. and Thomas L. (1991) *Learning Conversations*, Routledge, London.
9   For the conferencing approach to teaching writing see: Graves, D. (1983) *Writing*, Heinemann, London; for a conferencing approach to reading see: Arnold, H. (1983) *Listening to Children Reading*, Hodder & Stoughton, London.
10   van Ments, M. (1990) *Active Talk: The Effective use of Discussion in Learning*, Kogan Page, London.
11   'Community of enquiry' is a term used to describe philosophical discussion, and adopted by Matthew Lipman to describe the process employed in his Programme of Philosophy for Children. See Reference 12.
12   Dillon, J. T. (1994) *Using Discussion in Classrooms*, Open University Press, Buckingham, p. 30. Dillon argues that this form of discussion (as open enquiry) is the only genuine form of discussion and his book presents a useful overview of research on the theory and practice of discussion in schools.
13   Bridges, D. (1979) *Education, Democracy and Discussion*, NFER, Windsor.
14   For a discussion of intellectual virtues see Sutcliffe, R. (1993) 'Is Philosophical Enquiry Virtuous?', *Aspects of Education, no. 49*, a special issue on Socratic Education.
15   For a summary of some findings learnt from the National Oracy Project see Norman, K. (1991) 'The Teacher Effect', *Language and Learning*, vol. 8.
16   Ibid.
17   Edwards, D. and Mercer, N. (1987), *Common Knowledge*, Methuen, London.
18   Feuerstein, R. (1980) *Instrumental Enrichment: An Intervention Program for Cognitive Modifiability*, Scott, Foresman & Co., Glenview, Ill.
19   Andrews, R., Costello, P. and Clarke, S. (1993) *Improving the Quality of Argument*, University of Hull, Hull, pp. 5–16.
20   Ibid.
21   Fisher, R. (1990) *Teaching Children to Think*, Simon & Schuster, Hemel Hempstead,

pp. 155–184.

22 *Harry Stottlemeier's Discovery* by Matthew Lipman and was first published in 1974 by the Institute for the Advancement of Philosophy for Children, based at Montclair College, New Jersey, USA, together with a support manual for teachers entitled *Philosophical Enquiry* by Lipman, M., Sharp, A. M. and Oscanyan, F. S. in 1979. A version of this novel and manual adapted for use by British teachers has been produced by Roger Sutcliffe in 1993.

23 Oakeshott, M. (1967) 'Learning and Teaching', in Peters, R. S. (ed.) *The Concept of Education*, Routledge, London.

5 Cognitive mapping

Creating mind maps can help organise thinking and learning

As any photographer knows, the frame of the viewfinder 'organises' the image within it, creating a visual statement where, without the frame, one might see only clutter. And, as any builder knows, the frame of a building supports its totality. Both metaphors highlight a crucial feature of thinking frames. They support and organise thought, but they do not do the thinking. They are guides, not recipes.
David Perkins[1]

When you make a map it helps you to think about what you know and what you don't know.
Student, aged eleven

A map is a useful guide to where we are and where we wish to go. A map is a useful geographical tool. It is a way of making our thinking about space and location visible, showing us the interrelationships of places. We carry within us many mental maps that help us find our way round the locations we know and locations where we have never been.[2] Maps can be pictorial or made with symbols (usually printed maps are both pictorial and symbolic). Maps can also be made out of words, ideas and concepts. These can be called cognitive maps, and they can be powerful tools for learning.

Cognitive maps go under a variety of names. They are known as concept mapping, semantic mapping, knowledge mapping, word webbing, networking, clustering, mind-maps, think-links, idea branches, structured overviews or graphic organisers.[3] All such processes that involve the diagramming of thinking can be called cognitive maps. Cognitive maps attempt, visually and graphically, to portray a relationship of ideas or concepts. They are sometimes called concept maps because identifying key words and concepts makes it easier for us to use language, not only to make study notes but also in thinking, learning and remembering.

Memory is primarily a process of making links, connections and associations between new information and existing patterns of knowledge. Memory depends in large part on key words and key concepts that, when properly remembered, are transferred from short-term memory into long-term memory. It is through the linking of information to existing patterns of knowledge that we create new forms of understanding. If we cannot identify key words and concepts, and have not created patterns of understanding then our understanding and our memory become fragmentary – we have not grasped things, we have not created an effective map. In a sense all our knowledge is fragmentary, our understandings are partial. Like in fifteenth-century maps of the world there may be large areas of ignorance and incomprehension in our understanding of things. However, there is some terra firma, some firm foundations in our knowledge. We can show this by making our thinking visible through words, numbers, pictures etc. and through mapping concept words. Why concept words, and not sentences?

We have become so used to speaking and writing in sentences that we could easily assume that sentence structure is the best way of learning and remembering verbal images and ideas. In recalling information we rarely use a word-for-word verbatim process, we do not re-read from memory what we have learnt. This would be a very long and demanding process. It would be like having to learn and remember play-scripts all the time. We are able to access so many memories because all we need is to remember the key ideas, words or images and we re-create what we remember from these. When people describe a story, event or idea they usually extract the key elements and weave them into a fresh re-creation. Exceptions to this are when specific scripts have been learnt, as in joke-telling – though often here memory will rely on key phrases and images, and the tale will vary in the telling. This is why gossip (and many sorts of news-gathering) is often unreliable in its details. Memory is selective and episodic. We can research this with children through the use of memory games.

TASK 20

Memory games
The following games can serve as an investigation and stimulus for thinking about how memory works.

Chinese whispers
1 Put children into some continuous order, such as a circle or line.
2 Whisper a message into the first child's ear, so that others cannot hear.
3 Each child then passes the message they heard to the next child until the message runs from the first to last child.
4 Compare the message that went 'in' to the one that came 'out' at the end of the line.
5 Try messages of different complexity.
6 Discuss why the repeated message might have changed.

Secret stories
1 Go with a child out of the room, and tell a story.
2 A second child goes out of the room to hear the story recounted by the first child.
3 The first child returns. A third child goes out to hear the story from the second child.
4 The second child returns, a fourth goes out and so on.
5 After a given number of turns, when the last child is out of the room tell the original version, and invite the last child in to tell the last version as she or he heard it.
6 Compare versions and discuss. Do you think that there are ways of helping you to remember better?

The world is filled with a rich multiplicity of objects and experiences. We make order out of the world through transforming our perceptions (what we see, hear, feel etc.) into concepts (words and ideas). We are greatly helped in this process by sharing our experiences and ideas with others. A concept is an organising idea, it is an abstraction that pulls together a lot of facts, attempting to make sense of them by organising them into categories or classes. Concepts help us to classify and order thoughts and experiences, providing the labels that we give to these patterns of ideas. For instance, the scientific taxonomy (category system) for animals on our planet uses concepts such as class, order, family and species to organise our thinking about the creatures we have identified. Concepts group certain facts together to make distinctions and relationships between things. They express patterns of similarities and differences that organise and help to explain experience. They are constructions of the human mind that enable us to make sense of and to learn from experience.

Concepts are the labels we give for ideas that may be simple, such as dog and cat, or that may have complex layers of meaning, such as democracy and revolution. To understand a concept well, it is not sufficient to be given a dictionary or textbook definition. Many concepts have a variety of definitions that help explain the meaning of the ideas contained in the word. Another key aspect of understanding a concept is to be able to see what is and what is not an example of it. Skilled teachers combine these two processes of giving explanations and examples with a third process – that of helping the child to come to a communicative understanding of the concept (see Figure 5.1).

Explanations are important since children often have an incomplete grasp of what adults mean when they give a label to things. Examples are important, for children will often misapply concepts, such as the young child who calls geese and swans 'ducks' because they are duck-shaped. We

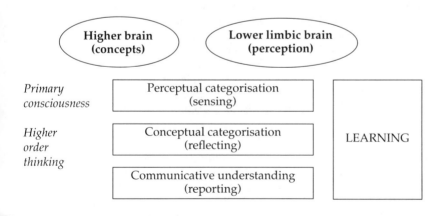

Figure 5.1 Conceptual understanding (adapted from Edelman[4])

do not know, however, even after careful explanations and examples, whether a concept has been assimilated into a child's wider knowledge of the world until we ask the child to represent and to share what they know. Creating a thinking map (or concept map) is one way of representing and communicating their understanding of concepts.

The understanding of a concept can vary enormously between children. What the concept of a colour or number is to a three-year old is very different to what it is to a ten-year old. A nursery teacher may talk of a child 'knowing his colours' when he knows, for example, what is green. The older child will have a fuller understanding of what green is, such as it can be made from yellow and blue, and knows many more examples of 'greenness'. He may know that 'green' is also an abstract term referring to environmental issues. However, his understanding may not be perfect. He may find it difficult to identify green in a painting of the sea, or know that green can be a symbol of jealousy. So learning a concept is not an 'all or nothing' process, it is the building up of successive approximations, of finer distinctions, of a widening network of related ideas, of coming closer to the common understandings of a culture and to the knowledge structure of experts. We increase our understanding by constructing and developing a wider network of meanings.

We make meaning by creating links between words and ideas. We learn more by making more links, by exploring and by testing links. The following task illustrates and provides practice in this process of connecting words and ideas.

TASK 21

Making connections

You may like to try these tasks on yourself before trying them with children.

Random words

1 Ask children to suggest any interesting word that comes into their minds.
2 Collect about twelve words, and display them on a board.
3 They think about the words and try to pair up any two words with a linking idea, e.g. head/hat (hats go on heads).
4 Try to find pairs of words in this way, or trios, e.g. horse/feet/helicopter (means of transport), or larger sets or families of words. Work individually or with a partner, allow thinking time, share findings with the group. A possible extension is to try to link all the words in an interesting story or explanatory narrative.

Topic words

1 List, or ask children to suggest, the dozen or so most important words on a chosen topic, e.g. Ancient Egypt, pond life or time. As above ask the children to think about the words and try to link them together with a connecting idea or ideas. These can be discussed or displayed in visual form.

'Only connect', said E. M. Forster. Making connections is the way we create an understanding of the world, and is the basic process of all creative thinking.

Are there any two words or concepts that cannot be linked in the mind with some sort of connecting idea? Descartes suggested that if we knew everything there was to know about anything we would have found out everything there was to know about everything. There is a sense in which all knowledge is threads within a seamless robe. We are just not aware of all the hidden links and connections. We are always in a state of incomplete knowledge, of coming to know, of building on our partial understandings. Throughout life, we are (or should be) constantly developing our conceptual understanding of the world.

Concept development

Vygotsky identified two levels of concept development. The first level is where concepts are spontaneously developed through perceptual and practical experience in everyday activity. These concepts are developed through rich experiences, but they are unsystematic and relate to particular human contexts. The higher level are 'scientific' concepts which are theoretical and structured, and depend on the use of language and learning. Concepts are either:

- spontaneous *learned through direct sensory experience such as learning what an orange is through touch, taste, sight etc., or*
- scientific *abstracted from experience and learned through language, for example, that all oranges have certain common elements such as 'roundness'.*

Scientific or abstract concepts are powerful because they can be applied to different contexts and fields of learning. They can be translated into increased abstraction, awareness and control of thought. These more advanced concepts can easily be cut off from experience and become unconnected with the concepts of everyday life. Hence the need for explanation – explanation from others (learning) and explanation to others (communication). The use of examples helps to embed knowledge in a human context. The use of explanation linked to examples is inductive reasoning and the basis of scientific method.

There are different levels of explanation, for example:

- labelling *giving no explanation, 'things just are', e.g. 'this is an orange'*
- enumerating *giving odd facts, 'this is what they are', e.g. 'there are oranges in shops'*
- making a link *pairing contiguous ideas, e.g. 'oranges grow on trees'*
- identifying common characteristics *e.g. similarities, 'oranges are round, have an orange colour, have pips' etc.*
- identifying concepts as belonging to a class *knowing class name, e.g. 'oranges are fruit/food'*
- identifying concepts as belonging to a pattern or hierarchy of concepts relating to other classes *e.g. orange as fruit/food/plant/living thing*
- identifying concepts as relating to other patterns of concepts *identifying similarities/differences with other classes, e.g. orange related to linguistic, mathematical, scientific, historical, geographical, economic and other conceptual patterns.*

Piaget argued that concepts are organised into 'schemas' or 'models' which are mental representations of things or ideas, and it is through these that we process information. For Piaget, cognitive development was very much to do with conceptual development, and this was often best achieved through cognitive conflict when our existing concepts or 'schemas' are challenged and our existing ideas disturbed. To learn is to change. Cognitive development must entail some change, some re-arrangement or enlargement of the conceptual structure. It is these conceptual structures that underlie skills and understanding. Cognitive mapping is one way that we can try to make visible a conceptual structure, not simply to see what it is, but to process it, to challenge it and to help enlarge it.

Concepts change and become more complex over time, and this process of conceptual development is helped by sharing our understandings and being challenged by the thoughts of others. One way of sharing an understanding of a concept is to list characteristics, and compare, contrast or discuss our ideas with others. For this any concept can be chosen – one that is in the news, one that is under study, one chosen by a child and so on. It can be a simple concept like 'tree' or 'wet', or something more complex like 'anger' or 'democracy'.

> **TASK 22**
>
> **Listing characteristics**
> This can begin as a group or class activity, as a paired or individual activity.
> It presents that most basic of problem-solving strategies – consider all factors, list all characteristics, find out what you know/find out what others know, and define the concept.
> 1 Choose a concept word.
> 2 Write it on a board, large piece of paper or overhead projector.
> 3 Ask the group to give as many characteristics/definitions as possible of the concept word.
> 4 List all suggestions.
> 5 After listing discuss similarities and differences. Could they be grouped into an order?

Concept mapping

How do you introduce children to the language of concepts? One way is to describe concepts as any word that means something, for example, names of people, places, things, events, ideas. It can help to say that a concept is a word which you can picture in the mind, not a linking word like 'and', 'but' or 'here'. We might say that a concept word has some connotation – it means something. Some words have no connotation, they merely act as connectors with other words, for example, 'the', 'an', 'and'. It is not always clear what a concept word is, or if a fixed meaning can be given to all, or any, words. Must all concepts be clear and open to definition, or are some concepts 'fuzzy' and never fully defined? Who defines what words or concepts mean? Philosophers have argued about the nature of concepts for centuries.

Children too can partake in this discussion, at their own level and for the purpose of coming to their own understanding.

The best way to begin introducing concept maps to children is to construct some of your own, first with general topics such as animals or vehicles, then with topics of study in school. The mapping of a subject should help you to think more clearly about it. When you have practised the process you may wish to introduce your pupils to the process. One way of generating initial concept maps with children is set out below.

Generating initial concept maps

1　Invite children to close their eyes and ask them if they can see a picture in their mind when you say a familiar word for an object, such as dog, chair or grass. Print these on the board and ask children for more examples.
2　Children now close their eyes and see a picture while you say an event word such as raining, running or painting. Ask children for more examples, and write them on the board.
3　Explain that words have meaning for us if we can see them as pictures in the mind. Try a few unfamiliar words to see if they can picture them in the mind. (If you have bilingual pupils you might try to introduce a few familiar 'foreign' words to show that people use different labels for the same meaning).
4　Introduce the word 'concept' and explain it is a way of describing a word that can be pictured in the mind. Review some words on the board to see if they are concept words.
5　Write some linking words such as the, is, are, when, that, then. Ask if these words bring pictures to the mind. Explain that these are not concept words but words that link concepts in sentences. Ask for more examples of linking words.
6　Ask the children to read some sentences from a book and to identify the concept words and linking words.
7　Ask children to pick a concept word, and begin to list information (brainstorm) about the word as a preparation for making their own concept maps.

The following tasks can help them to explore what concept words are.

TASK 23

Thinking maps

Brainstorming
1　Choose a concept word, for example, 'spiders' and ask children to list all the words they can think of connected with 'dogs' (see Figure 5.1). What words do they list?
2　Compare their list with a partner. What words are the same, and different? Share with the whole group.
This task is a useful pre-writing, or pre-mapping exercise.

Concept mapping
1 After brainstorming/listing words connected to a concept write the concept word in the middle of the board or a page.
2 Link the connected words to the central concept word with lines.
3 Write along the lines the relationship between the concept and connected words.

Mapping a text
1 Give each pair of children a page from a reading or text-book(a text of between 10 and 30 sentences). Ask them to list or mark every concept word they can find.
2 How often does the same concept word appear? Which concept word appears most often? Which are the most important concept words (which words could you not leave out for the passage to still make sense?).
3 List or mark words that are not concepts, that do not mean anything by themselves.
4 Share and discuss.

Listing words and concepts is a useful activity, it encourages fluency and flexibility of ideas, and provides a good basis for writing or for further classification. However, many people find it easier to take in information which is presented in a non-linear form. The brain works in complex patterns which are integrated and interlinked. We are used to receiving information from the world, from pictures and television in non-linear visual patterns. In nature there are no straight lines. Some of us prefer to think in straight lines, as observation of suburban gardens and the pattern-making of children show. Others prefer a more organic visual stimulus, rather than traditional 'lines'.

In a concept map (or mind-map) a key word or concept is one that is linked to many others, and serves as a focal point for making connections with other parts in the pattern. A key concept in the study of nature might be 'animal' or 'plant', and each of these could be linked to a family of related concepts (see Figures 5.2 and 5.3). A pattern working out from the centre of a main idea has a number of advantages in that:

- the central, main or key idea is clearly defined
- the relative importance of ideas can be clearly shown by being highlighted, or put nearer the centre
- links between ideas can be clearly shown
- visual patterning allows for easy overview and review
- the structure is provisional and organic, allowing for additions and adaptations
- the open-ended nature of the process encourages the making of connections between ideas
- each pattern is individual and unique, making it easier to remember, recall and repeat.

The first stage is often the brainstorming of ideas and connections. An important feature of thinking maps is that the *connecting ideas* are made explicit, either through discussion or through being written along the line that connects the concept words. It is the making of connections visible or explicit that differentiates thinking maps from the simple brainstorming of ideas. The process can be an important aid to learning. Once it has been tried in a class or group with others it can become a learning tool to be used whenever needed and for a variety of purposes. What purposes can this think-mapping serve?

The purposes of cognitive mapping

Cognitive mapping can serve a number of purposes. Three of the main aims or purposes of making thinking visible though cognitive mapping (think-mapping, mind-mapping or concept mapping) are:

- to explore what we know *identifying the key concepts, showing links between ideas and making a meaningful pattern out of what we know and understand*[5] (see Figures 5.2 and 5.3)
- to help planning *as an aid to planning an activity or project by organising and grouping ideas and showing links between them* (see Figure 5.4)
- to aid evaluation *helping the evaluation of experience or knowledge through a process of reflection on the key elements of what we know or have done* (see Figures 5.2 and 5.3).

Cognitive maps can provide children with a means to articulate their ideas. They provide a tool for planning and assessing or evaluating what they know. They stimulate active thinking, develop cognitive skills of analysis, categorisation and synthesis, and provide a visual means for communication and evaluation. A major benefit of mapping is that we can use this practical, visually oriented strategy within the context of any topic in the school curriculum. There are a number of different map structures that can help students to represent and organise what they know and can find out. Mapping strategies can allow teachers to cover topics in greater depth, where meanings can be found and created in an organised and ongoing way. A map design can be displayed on a board or transferred onto a transparency and projected onto a screen, that can be viewed, adapted and developed over time. Mapping provides a framework which can be added to, over time. Mapping provides a whole language framework in which all the areas of language skill – speaking, listening, reading and writing, can be used in meaningful ways.

Rather than supporting a passive teaching/learning environment, mapping encourages children to be actively engaged in thinking, to elaborate and build on ideas. They not only receive information, but need to re-think it, interpret it and relate it to their schemas of understanding. Mapping can help information flow to, from and among pupils and teachers. Most importantly children learn a procedure for investigating, visualising and organising information. Learning to organise ideas is an important pre-writing strategy,[6] and is an important study skill in helping to understand the structure of any text they read.[7] Mapping can be used in all curriculum areas.[8] In addition, with mapping, pupils and teachers

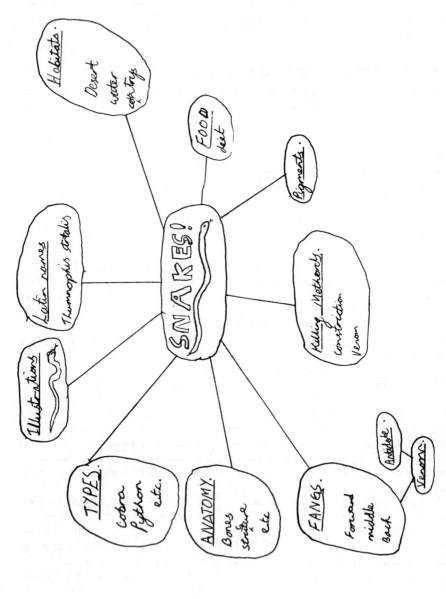

Figure 5.2 A cognitive map of a project about snakes

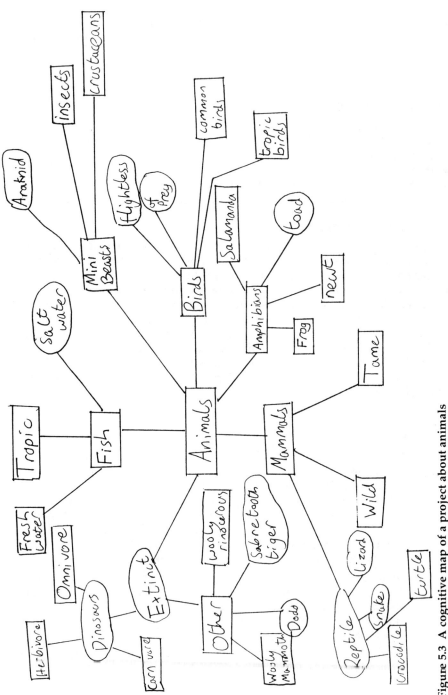

Figure 5.3 A cognitive map of a project about animals

have the opportunity to use computers to reinforce the skills of both mapping and of learning curriculum content; because mapping is a highly visual and spatial activity, the computer is an excellent medium to display a network of visual information. What then are the forms that think-mapping can take?

Forms of mapping

A map visually consists of an arrangement of shapes such as boxes, circles, rectangles, triangles etc., connected by lines and/or arrows drawn between and among the figures. The map conceptually contains verbal information within and between the shapes to create a pattern or relationships of ideas. The aim of the map is to show how the whole topic in question can be portrayed. There are several forms that this mapping can take.

Hierarchical concept mapping

Simple concept maps create a semantic web from a simple idea or key concept. A more advanced strategy is to map concepts into a hierarchical form. A hierarchical concept map shows pupils how to represent a hierarchy of ideas within a given topic and to show the relationships between them. Research shows that children as young as five years can create hierarchical concept maps of a simple kind, but it is not usually until around ten years that children produce maps that show quality and complexity of thinking – and it is around this age that some teachers have found group work on hierarchical concept mapping to be most beneficial.[9]

The following are some tasks to help develop children's understanding of concept mapping.

TASK 24

Hierarchical concept mapping

Listing hierarchies

1 Make a list of ten or twelve words related to a concept, e.g. seaweed, plankton, fish, shark, plants, mammals, shoals, coral, whales, waves, tides.
2 Ask children to guess the concept that relates to all the words, e.g. sea.
3 Build a concept map by organising the concept words from the more general to the more specific concepts in a visual hierarchy.
4 Ask children to add words, and show cross links if they can.

Creating hierarchical maps

1 List words on a chosen concept, e.g. dogs. Ask children to rank them from the most general to the most particular, e.g. animals, four-legged, canine, dogs, wild/domestic etc.
2 Ask children to create their own hierarchical concept maps.
   Give several lists and let the children choose which list they want to map.

Mapping stories

1 Choose a familiar story or excerpt from a story.
2 Help them to prepare a list of concepts from the story.

3 Reorganise the list from the most important to the least important in the story.
4 Discuss the list and help them create a concept map from the story.

Mapping chosen topics
1 Ask children to prepare a concept map on any topic, e.g. sport, hobby they knows well.
2 Display/share maps, encouraging positive comments.

Knowledge maps

Staring at a textbook is one of the most inefficient ways of learning facts. It is when we are actively processing the facts, doing something with them, that they are likely to stay in the memory. Creating a knowledge map is a technique that can work well when there are a lot of facts to learn, as in science, geography or history.

Here is one way of helping a young child or group of children to create a knowledge map.

1 Provide some plain cards, e.g. postcards, some coloured pens and reference materials such as a textbook, a reference book, lesson notes or a computer database.
2 Select twelve (or more) different facts on a topic of research and write each one on a card using as few words as possible, and using different colours for the words, drawings, numbers etc.
3 Lay out the fact cards on a table or floor. Arrange them in any shape you wish e.g. tree, circle, line, ladder etc. so they make a connecting pattern.
4 Play a memory game. Turn all the cards over, except one. Ask children to test each other. Can they choose a card, and remember what it says? Check by turning over the card.
5 Display and discuss the knowledge map design, e.g. by gluing the cards onto a chart, or by keeping the cards loose, e.g. in a file so that pupils can experiment with different map designs and can add more fact cards to the collection.

Graphic organisers

Children should be introduced to a variety of ways of organising information in graphic form. In having experience of different ways of mapping information they will have a means of processing any information for better understanding, but also will be able to utilise their preferred way of making thinking maps. Research shows that there is no one way that is best or which suits all people. Some prefer a linear arrangement, some geometric forms, others more free flowing organic structures. This has a lot to do with individual learning style, as well as the experience of the learner. Which ways of organising thinking have you tried? Which suit you best?

Graphic organisers and other forms of cognitive mapping can provide a good focus for co-operative learning and can engage students in the shared processing of information and ideas in many ways.

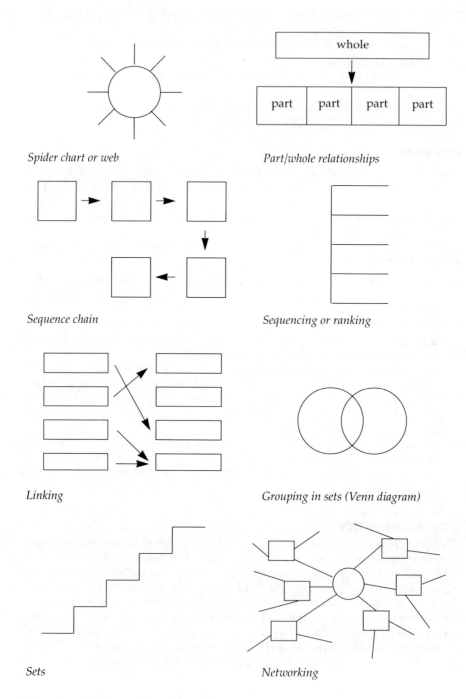

Spider chart or web

Part/whole relationships

Sequence chain

Sequencing or ranking

Linking

Grouping in sets (Venn diagram)

Sets

Networking

Figure 5.4 Some graphic organisers

Ways in which graphic organisers can help students include:

- using cognitive mapping as a group activity to create a common frame of reference for thinking
- using a cognitive map as a tangible outcome of group discussion.

Cognitive mapping will not only help students to remember more, and provide opportunities for 'higher order' processing of information, it also provides opportunities for shared and co-operative thinking that can be both stimulating and enjoyable. The use of cognitive mapping can teach students how to shape, organise and communicate their thinking. As one child put it: 'I like seeing what I think, and I like seeing what others think.' Another added: 'It is easier to show what you think than to say what you think.' A third said: 'It gives you a chance to see what you think first and to think about it afterwards.' Wherever they want to go, or whatever they need to learn, knowing how to make a map could help them to find their way.

Summary

Cognitive mapping can be a powerful aid to memory, understanding and concept development. Concepts are organising ideas that help us make sense of the world, and a child's learning is developed through organising information and ideas into patterns and frameworks of understanding. Graphic organisers and other cognitive mapping strategies help students to represent thinking in visual form, to depict relationships between facts and concepts, and relate new information to prior knowledge. Mapping can take many forms and be used to support a wide range of contexts for learning. Cognitive mapping can also provide a focus for group discussion and be a means to facilitate co-operative learning.

References

1   Quote from Perkins, D. N. (1987) 'Thinking Frames: An Integrating Perspective on Teaching Cognitive Skills', in Baron, J. and Sternberg, R. *Teaching Thinking Skills: Theory and Research*, W. H. Freeman, New York.
2   For more on the way we create mental maps of places we know, see: Gould, P. and White, R. (1986) *Mental Maps*, (2nd edn), Allen & Unwin, London.
3   The following offer useful guidance on the theory and practice of mapping thinking:
    Buzan, T. (1974) *Use Your Head*, BBC Publications, London;
    Novak, J. D. and Gowin, D. B. (1984) *Learning How to Learn*, Cambridge University Press, Cambridge;
    Clarke, J. (1990) *Patterns of Thinking: Integrating Learning Skills in Content Teaching*, Allyn & Bacon, Boston;
    Schwartz, R. and Parks, S. (1994) *Infusing the Teaching of Critical and Creative Thinking into Elementary Instruction*, Critical Thinking Press, Pacific Grove, Cal.
4   Edelman, G. (1992) *Bright Air, Brilliant Fire*, Penguin, Harmondsworth.
5   Ausubel argued that all learning should begin with finding out what the student already knows. Cognitive mapping is a useful technique for this 'bringing

to mind'. See Ausubel, D. (1968) *Educational Psychology: A Cognitive View*, Holt, Rinehart & Winston, New York.

6   Doyle, R. (1986) *Webbing as a Prewriting Strategy*, Maryland Writing Project, Baltimore.

7   Sinatra, R. (1990) 'Semantic Mapping: A Thinking Strategy for Improved Reading and Writing Development', *Teaching Thinking and Problem Solving*, vol. 12, no. 1, Jan–Feb, Lawrence Erlbaum Associates, Hillsdale.

8   For the use of mapping in science teaching see: Kilshaw, J. (1990) 'Using Concept Maps', *Primary Science Review*, vol. 12, Spring, pp. 34–6; and Chapter 9 in Harlen, W. (1993) *Teaching and Learning Primary Science*, Paul Chapman, London.

9   Stice, C. F. and Alvarez, M. C. (1987) 'Hierarchical Concept Mapping in the Early Grades', *Childhood Education*, October.

6 Divergent thinking

Creative thinking can help children make learning their own

To him whose elastic and vigorous thought keeps pace with the sun, the day is perpetual morning.
Henry Thoreau

I learn best when I learn in my own way.
Child, aged nine

A class of young children were being taught about the importance of dental hygiene, and the risks that they might incur of needing to have false teeth when they were older. One of the children responded: 'My grandma doesn't need false teeth'. 'Do you know why not?' asked the teacher. 'Yes,' said the child, 'she's dead.'

We become creative when we are able to look at things from a new perspective. Einstein, who believed that the key to learning was flexible thinking, said: 'To raise new questions, new problems, to regard old problems from a new angle requires creative imagination, and makes real advances'. According to Piaget, 'to understand is to invent'.[1] We make knowledge our own 'by reconstructing it through some creative operation of the mind.' 'The mind once stretched by a new idea', said Oliver Wendell Holmes, 'never regains its original dimensions.'

Any learning that is not routine needs creativity. Unless the learner has complete knowledge of an area of learning, then creativity will be needed to help develop, adapt and apply understanding that is at present partial or incomplete. When knowledge is complete, we have no need to process it further, there is no need to think things through. To take account of new knowledge, develop new ideas, or design solutions to new problems requires creative thinking. Creative or divergent thinking offers the chance to see more in any situation.

One of the reasons that creativity is needed in learning is that intelligence alone is not sufficient to realise learning potential. Intelligent people are not necessarily successful at thinking and learning. They may fall into what Edward de Bono calls the 'intelligence trap' of making instant judgements, of jumping to conclusions, without taking time to think about and explore alternatives. They may close off the opportunities to think and learn more. This impulsivity, or tendency to premature closure, is a characteristic of under-achieving children at all levels of intelligence. Thinking is defined by de Bono as 'the operating skill with which intelligence acts upon experience'. One of the characteristics of skilful thinking is exploration, the ability to explore a situation before making a judgement. These thinking skills are not automatic, but they can be developed.[2]

Creativity, intelligence plus achievement

Creativity seems to be a capacity that is separate from intelligence, and the ways in which these combine can lead to very different learning styles and levels of achievement. Researchers have compared samples of children with high and low scores on tests to measure intelligence and on tests to measure creativity covering educational, psychological and social dimensions. Their findings are summarised as follows:[3]

- high creativity plus high intelligence *These children can exercise within themselves both control and freedom, both adult-like and child-like kinds of behaviour.*
- high creativity plus low intelligence *These children are in angry conflict with themselves and with their school environment and are beset with feelings of unworthiness and inadequacy. In a stress-free context, they can blossom forth cognitively.*
- low creativity plus high intelligence *These children can be described as 'addicted' to school achievement. Academic failure would be conceived by them as catastrophic, so that they must continually strive for academic excellence to avoid the possibility of pain.*
- low creativity plus low intelligence *Basically bewildered, these children engaged in various defensive social activities and regressions such as passivity or psychosomatic symptoms.*

Research suggests that creativity is an important element in the achievement of some children whatever their intelligence or social background, and that creative thinking and doing can help develop the potential both of individuals and of human institutions such as schools or commercial organisations. But how do we assess and develop creative thinking?

Assessing creative thinking

The mind is an attention-focusing device. We become creative when we can vary and extend the focus of attention, when we are able to see and think of possibilities beyond the given information. We construct, we invent, we play with ideas. We have different capacities for creative thinking, and these capacities can be expanded and developed through practice. Typically this kind of divergent thinking comes in focused bursts, in response to a stimulus. But how good are we, or our students, at creative thinking?

Various tests have been designed to practice and to assess levels of creative thinking. The following are examples of three kinds of test:

- a drawing test where students are asked to create a design from a simple given drawn shape or pattern
- a visualisation test where students are asked of a given drawing: 'What is it?' and try to list as many different possible items the drawing may be trying to represent
- a verbal test where students are asked, e.g. to generate creative ideas from a given verbal stimulus. 'How many uses can you think of for a ...?'.

Drawing test

The following example is from the Torrance Tests of Creative Thinking (figural section).[4]

1 Give each student a sheet of A4 with a set of 20 circles arranged in orderly lines on each side of the page, making a total of 40 circles.
2 Invite them to draw as many interesting and unusual things involving the use of a circle as they can in ten minutes. If necessary give an example, e.g. a self-portrait. How many different things can they draw?
3 Ask them to put a caption under each drawing (optional).

Torrance suggests this test can be used to assess what he identifies as the four dimensions of creative thinking:

- fluency *the number of different ideas generated. Assess this by counting the total number of different things that are drawn (a drawing can use just one or many circles)*
- flexibility *the number of different categories of ideas. Count the number of different categories used, e.g. ball/football/other balls would be one category*
- originality *the divergence of ideas from conventional or common choices. Score each drawing 0, 1 or 2 for originality. If everybody draws the same thing, e.g., a face, score 0, if only a few draw it, e.g., a screw, score 1, if only one person draws it, e.g., a lamp base, score 2. The total score is the originality rating*
- elaboration *the detailed expression of ideas. Assess the amount of detail given in each picture. This is very difficult to mark objectively.*

Ask students to give themselves a score for fluency and flexibility, to identify their most original ideas and to compare across the group. Torrance found that high scores in originality and elaboration gave the highest correlation with creative ability. He also found some very individual creative responses did not score highly on these measures, such as those of a child who incorporated all the circles into a bee's honeycomb!

Visualisation test

What is a visualisation test?

Figure 6.1 is an example of a visualisation test. Look at the shape below and list as many things as you can think of that it might represent.

Figure 6.1 An example of a visualisation test

The suggestions from a group of children in response to this test included: sun, moon, star, light, torch, light, octopus, raindrop, well, spider's web, wheel, water splash, dandelion, volcano, explosion, firework, hair rising, button, bell, seed, bullet-hole, bottle top, loudspeaker, moon crater, satellite, compass, eye, jet engine, ring, fountain, electricity, cog, water wheel, flower head, squashed spider, happiness, roads, head-dress of the Statue of Liberty and legs sticking out from under a parasol.

Verbal test

How many uses?

An example of a verbal test of divergent thinking would be a question like: How many alternative uses as can you think of for a familiar object such as a blanket, barrel, brick, sock, paper clip, a shoebox, an elastic band, a human hair, toothbrush, compact disc, milk bottle, sock etc.?

These tests can be conducted with students from age eight to adults, but its use in identifying creative potential is highly debatable. Such tests can, however, provide a useful focus for exercising creativity, and for discussing creativity and the criteria used for judging it. In this kind of test there is no right answer, assessment is subjective and tests or re-tests often produce widely diverse scores.

Developing creative thinking

Torrance suggests that creativity is 'a process of becoming sensitive to problems, deficiencies, gaps in knowledge, missing elements, disharmonies, and so on; identifying the difficulty; searching for solutions, making guesses, or formulating hypotheses about the deficiencies, testing and retesting these hypotheses and possibly modifying and retesting them; and finally communicating the results'.

Creativity is a form of intelligence that can be trained and developed like any other mode of thinking. It is not merely a question of playing with things, of randomness or chance, but, at its best, has to do with serious and sustained effort in thinking about any area of learning.

The most widely used creative thinking programme is Edward de Bono's CoRT Thinking,[5] which consists of a number of 'tools' applicable to a wide range of teaching situations. The tools are simple but powerful strategies for getting students to think more widely, to promote deeper reflection, and to avoid impulsivity. They represent a systematic summary of the most productive strategies in developing divergent thinking. The following is a brief overview of seven of the 'tools' and their acronyms devised by de Bono for his CoRT programme.

CoRT thinking tools

CAF	Consider All Factors
FIP	First Important Priorities
PMI	Plus, Minus, Interesting points
C & S	Consequences and Sequel
AGO	Aims, Goals and Objectives

APC   Alternative Possible Choices
OPV   Other Points of View

Consider all factors (CAF)

Creative thinking is about generating ideas and increasing the breadth of perception. Instead of a narrow focus we try to review the whole field. CAF is a tool which aims to expand the focus of attention. What factors should we consider in this situation? If we want children to have the ability to take in many things, things which are within the situation and things outside relevant to the situation, things now present and things that may happen in the future, children will need to have experience in broadening their perception, to look beyond the given, and to consider all factors.

In using CAF as a tool for learning, what is important is not simply the process of brainstorming ideas, but that we have an attention-directing tool that encourages thinking time. As with all tools, skill in use requires practice and familiarisation (for example by having the acronym written on a chart or bookmark). The more the tool is used in a deliberate manner the more useful the tool becomes by being internalised through practice.

My research with junior-age children shows that CAF, like other tools of de Bono, is quickly forgotten if used only once. But, if repeated in a variety of learning contexts over a period of time, it becomes a 'thinking frame' that is remembered and used.

- Can you do a CAF?
- Have you done a CAF?
- Should we do a CAF?

CAF is a simple tool, but is powerful if it is done well. It is an ideal strategy for when you have to choose or make a decision, for it encourages you to withold judgement and to reflect on all factors. The following tasks can provide practice in the use of the CAF technique.

TASK 25

Considering all factors

On your own, or with a partner, make a list of factors for each of the following:
1 Your family have decided to move to a new home. What factors should they take into account in deciding on a new home?
2 You are choosing a summer holiday. What factors should you keep in mind?
3 What factors make for a good teacher?
4 What makes for a good story? List all the factors that might be included in writing a good story.
5 You are designing a chair. What factors should you take into account?

First important priorities (FIP)

FIP is simply a prioritising tool which directs the attention to thinking about priorities. Not all factors are of equal importance. Some things are more important than others, some values are more important than others. Priorities are things that should be taken into account in planning and reviewing what has or should be done.

- Are there a lot of things that are important?
- Which are most important?
- What are the priorities?
- Are your priorities the same or different from mine or other people's?

In reviewing a list of factors, for example, in choosing a holiday, we may think that all the factors are priorities – and a case can be made for the importance or value of most things. The role of FIP (or any prioritising strategy) is that it forces us to make choices and to decide what the really important things to consider should be.

In doing a prioritising exercise it is useful to set a limit on the number of priorities, for example, three, four or five. The above CAF tasks can be extended to consider what are the most important priorities in each list.

The task below provides further opportunities for considering priorities.

TASK 26

Deciding priorities

Make a list of factors and then prioritise three or four items in order of importance.

1. In choosing a friend what are your first most important priorities?
2. A sum of £1000 has been given to improve your school. What would be your priorities in spending the money?
3. What do you think are the most important factors in choosing to buy a new bicycle?
4. What rules should a school or class have? Which are the most important?
5. What should parents consider in choosing a school for their child? Which are the most important points to consider?

Deciding on priorities can be used in all learning contexts which require planning, analysing or evaluating. For example, in studying *Romeo and Juliet*, students might analyse the couple's decision to marry by considering all factors (CAF) and, then, prioritise the factors that lead to the decision (FIP). After prioritising the factors, students could then consider each factor in terms of its advantages, disadvantages and points of interest (a strategy de Bono calls PMI).

Plus, minus, interesting points (PMI)

'Think before you leap,' says de Bono, and PMI is a strategy that aims to force us into thinking about any situation before coming to a judgement about it. The process involves listing all the good points, bad points and interesting points about a given idea, object or event. It is one of the most effective tools for directing attention to and generating thinking about the different aspects of a particular topic.

'Plus' relates to the positive elements of the topic, 'Minus' to the negative elements, and 'Interesting' to those points that are neither good nor bad, but are regarded as neutral observations, comments or points of interest.

- I'm not sure about this, let's do a PMI.
- To find out more about what we think let us do a PMI.
- There are two options – let us do a PMI on each.

PMI is a useful evaluation tool that can be used to generate thinking about any situation or piece of work. Pictures, objects or texts can be subjected to creative analysis using the PMI method. The following are examples of activities with which to practice divergent thinking using PMI.

TASK 27

Assessing positive, negative and interesting points
Make a list for each category of good points under 'Plus', bad points under 'Minus', and 'Interesting' points about a given topic.
1 Attendance at school should not be compulsory for any child.
2 People should wear badges to show if they are in a good or bad mood that day.
3 All seats should be taken out of buses.
4 Think about what you have done today, yesterday or during the last week. What were the positive, negative and interesting points in your life during this time?
5 Choose a book, picture or television film and do a PMI on it.

Consequences and sequel (C & S)

All our actions and decisions have consequences. Often these consequences go unconsidered. As Socrates said, many of us lead 'unexamined lives'. In considering a course of action, for ourselves or by others, we need to consider the consequences. Young children are egocentric, they think primarily of themselves, and they live in the present and find it difficult to project themselves into the future. Considering the consequences invites children to speculate, and to predict along a time scale into the future.

Consequences occur along a time scale which can be:

- immediate *what may happen as an immediate consequence*
- short term *what may soon happen in a short period of time*
- medium term *what may happen after some time when things have settled down*
- long term *what may happen much later.*

Important concepts of possibility, probability and certainty are involved in considering questions like those listed below.

- What outcome are you sure about?
- Will it always turn out like this?

- What else could it be like?
- Do we know what will happen?
- What do you think will happen? Why?

Part of assessing possible consequences is working out not only what will happen, but also the risks involved – what might upset our prediction and alter the consequences.

- What are the dangers?
- What might go wrong?
- What is the worst thing that could go wrong?
- What is the ideal (best) outcome?
- What is the most likely outcome?

Here are some activities to encourage consideration of consequences.

TASK 28
Considering the consequences
Make a list of consequences for each of the topics below. Specify a time scale for each consequence, for example, less than a year, 1–5 years, 5–15 years, or over 25 years.
1 The discovery of America by European explorers.
2 The invention of computers.
3 The world runs out of oil.
4 The greenhouse effect makes the earth's atmosphere much warmer than at present.
5 Scientists discover a cure for every known illness.

Sequels also provide good starting points for divergent thinking. A question like: What do you think will happen next? could refer to the next page, episode, book, picture, design, action or idea. Begin a story and invite the child to continue it. Or invite the child to say what might have happened before a story, what happened in the past, during the antecedent period, what was the prequel? We can help children to think more widely in time, past (prequel), present and future (sequel), and more deeply at the causes and consequences of things. An understanding of these concepts is a gradual process but they can be powerful tools for understanding about how and why things change.

Aims, goals and objectives (AGO)

'Why are you doing this?' is a question we can ask of ourselves or others. When children are asked this question in school they often find it difficult to give a clear answer. The most common answer is 'because my teacher told me'. Children do things without knowing why. They inhabit an environment whose purpose is activity but they do not know the reasons for this activity. They live in a moment-to-moment world where the pattern and purpose of their learning is not clear. They often do not know the focus of their learning or the aim of their learning activity.

AGO is related to broadening perception by seeking to identify the purpose of our thinking and learning. Trying to explain the distinctions between 'aims', 'goals' and 'objectives' may not be time well spent. What is important is knowing what one is trying to achieve.

- What are we trying to do?
- What do we want to end up with?
- Why are we doing this?
- What is the purpose?
- What objective are we trying to achieve?

The following are some activities that focus on defining aims.

TASK 29

Defining the aims
Make a list of what you think the following may be trying to achieve.
1 A football team.
2 Someone in your group who is telling lies about you.
3 You are designing a new type of house. What are your aims?
4 Your parents, or your teacher.
5 You, in going to school.

Alternatives, possibilities, choices (APC)

The world is full of alternatives, possibilities and choices, but we do not always see them. This is especially true of the learning child, who often comes to believe there is only one answer, only one right way to do things. We need to be alert to alternatives, to possible new directions, and to have the courage to sometimes choose 'the road less travelled by'. We talk of being 'blinkered', and of 'tunnel vision'. As learners, we talk of 'getting stuck', and of not knowing what to do, where to turn, which way to go. If children value the practice of seeking alternatives they will be better placed to generate options when they need them.
  There are many sorts of alternatives:

- viewpoints *looking at the same thing in different ways, from other viewpoints*
- actions *seeing alternative possible courses of action in a given situation*
- solutions *being aware of alternative solutions to a problem*
- ways of working *realising that there are different ways of tackling a problem*
- explanations *suggesting alternative explanations and hypotheses to explain how something happened*
- plans *devising alternative plans for approaching a task*
- designs *creating alternative designs for meeting a need or purpose.*

Encourage children to look for alternatives, to be alert to the multiplicity of possibilities. Support the belief that they always have a choice. If one way does not work look for alternatives. If there seems to be only one way, look for alternatives. You may not find them, but your approach is intelligent. As one child commented: 'There is always a different way, even if you can't find it'.

The most difficult thing to do is to check and look for alternatives when you do not have to. We do things out of habit, we work mindlessly. What can help us to be more flexible in our thinking, and more alert to possibilities? The following are some questions that may help.

- Is there another way?
- Can we come up with an alternative suggestion?
- Is there a possibility we have not thought of?
- What other choices have we got?
- Have we considered all the options?

When we begin to look for alternatives we should be clear about the purpose of the alternative. The following tasks provide sample ways in which the process of looking for alternatives can be encouraged.

TASK 30

Seeking alternatives
Make a list of options, alternatives and possibilities to help in making a decision about the following problems or situations.
1 You discover your best friend is a thief. What alternatives do you have?
2 As you walk along the street you see a woman collapse to the ground. Why could this have happened? What could you do?
3 A car is found crashed in a ditch. There is no driver. What happened?
4 Some places are dirty because people drop litter and cans everywhere. What could you do to solve this problem?
5 You and your friends decide to raise money for charity. Which charity? What could you do?

Other points of view (OPV)

One way to broaden perception is to try to see things from another person's point of view. For the child, and perhaps for us all, this is a difficult challenge. It requires an ability to listen to the views expressed by other people, and to make an imaginative leap to understand their feelings and ideas. This leap of imagination is fundamental to moral development, and to an understanding of others (interpersonal intelligence).

An obvious way into thinking about other points of view is to consider both sides of an argument or conflict. It can be fruitful, when stopping a quarrel or fight between two children, to get each to state their own point of view without the other interrupting. Stories and drama also provide good opportunities to look at different points of view.

- Does everyone think the same thing?
- What do you think? What does she or he think?
- What do the others think?
- What are they feeling? Why?
- What do you think is going through his or her mind or their minds?

The following tasks encourage seeing things from another's point of view.

TASK 31

Recognising other points of view

List what you think the views are of different people in these examples:

1 A father and mother forbid their son and daughter to stay up past ten o'clock to watch a television programme they want to see. What are the different views of the parents, and children?

2 Someone wants to sell you a second-hand bicycle. What are their views, and your views?

3 You lend a friend some money to buy a lottery ticket. Your friend wins a prize with the ticket. Who does the prize belong to? What might be the different points of view of you and your friend?

4 A burglar breaks into your house and steals everything of value that can be found. Your parents call the police, who say they will try their best to catch the thief. What are the views of your parents, the burglar and the police?

5 Choose a book, picture or video programme and list the different thoughts, feelings and points of view of the characters.

Creative thinking can be learned and developed. All forms of study should allow for some use of creative, divergent or lateral thinking. 'You cannot dig a hole in a different place,' says de Bono, 'by digging the same hole deeper'. Trying harder with the same ideas and same approach may not solve the problem. This is especially so with those having trouble with learning. They may need to move laterally to try new ideas and a new approach. Lateral thinking includes a number of methods for escaping from established ideas in order to find new ones. Children should be given the chance to think in new ways – but how?

Provocation

One way is through provocation, what creative thinking guru Roger von Oech[6] calls 'a whack on the side of the head'. He argues that we need to be whacked out of habitual thought patterns and provoked to look at what you are doing in a new way. The word 'po' has been coined by de Bono to describe a similar kind of 'provocative operation'. One technique is what Victor Quinn calls 'provocation in role', which entails the teacher or other 'agent provocateur' playing the devil's advocate in discussion with children by challenging all or any received moral and scientific assumptions with a view to building up a child's confidence and resilience in argument. A provocative statement is any that will stimulate creative thought, response or discussion.

Examples of provocative statements might include.

- There is no point in going to school.
- Nothing is true.
- I can do whatever I want.
- A triangle can have four sides.
- Adults know more than children so what they say is never wrong.

What provocative statements can you create to get your children thinking and responding?

What if ...?

You see things and say, 'Why?' But I dream things and say, 'Why not?'
     G. B. Shaw

What if animals could speak? What if we could live forever? What if the earth stopped revolving and the sun did not arise? 'What ifs' provide a wishful thinking kind of provocation by adding some impossible feature or by picking out some feature of an item and imagining it was missing. The following are some examples of such statements.

- What essential features of the following could you imagine leaving out of – a house, school, bicycle, library, birthday? What if your house had no ...?
- What features could you imagine adding to – school, parents, clothes, sleep, sports – Wouldn't it be nice if ....?

Can you or your children create ten 'What if....' impossibilities. Choose, draw and discuss your most interesting idea.

Synectics – making the familiar strange

An important element in creative problem solving is making the familiar strange – looking at the same problem in different ways. Synectics research identified three methods of creating metaphor for helping to see the familiar in new ways.[7]

- direct analogy *making a simple comparison, for example, How is a teacher like a tuna sandwich?*
- personal analogy *imagining being the thing, for example, A candle is not alive, but it looks alive when it burns. How would you feel if you were a candle burning in a camping tent?*
- symbolic analogy *creating a compressed conflict (oxymoron), for example, What is an example of a careful collision?*

Carl Sandburg, the American poet, once said: 'Poetry is the synthesis of hyacinths and biscuits'. Here, he was taking two unrelated words or images and putting them together to make the familiar strange. One way of doing this is to take two unrelated words or ideas and try to join them with a linking thought. If we say that what we think about one thing is also true of another we are reasoning by analogy. Children can be encouraged to create an analogy by asking questions such as: What is similar to this object? How are they similar? What do you know about one object that might be true of the other?

Examples of students creating metaphors about themselves are:

- I am undiscovered gold lying in the hills, waiting to be discovered.
- I am like a grape, just one of a bunch, but I am full of juicy goodness.
- I am like a pawn in a game of chess, but without me the game would not work.

TASK 32

Creating metaphors

Think of as many answers as you like for these questions. There are no right or wrong answers.

1   What answers can you find for these riddles.
    Why is summer like a bridge?
    Which animal is like a rubber band?
    Which colour is quickest?
2   Create more metaphorical riddles of your own by linking two seemingly unrelated ideas.
3   Make up some metaphors (or analogies) about yourself.
    What kind of food are you?
    What kind of furniture are you?
    What kind of animal are you?
4   Think of some more categories, and make up some more metaphors.
5   Create some more metaphors about yourself.
    What is your mind/brain like?
    What is your life like?

Some ideas for activities that can help develop creative thinking are set out below.

Link-ups

Choose any word. Write it down. Look at it and write the first word that comes into your head that is somehow associated with it. Continue to add words, building up a sequence of associations. See how long you can keep the chain going. Or say the words out loud while your partner scribes them. A more challenging version of this activity is to try to reach in a chain of association a very different word from the first word.

Picture this

Choose a reproduction of a painting. Write any words that come into your mind when you look at the picture. Try weaving a story round the image. Describe the picture without showing it to your partner. Can they visualise it? Visualise a picture that they describe, and draw it from their description.

Picture construction

Scatter dots over a page. Reproduce several copies. Create pictures using the dots as starting points.

Story ending

Any problem can have several solutions, so, therefore, any story can have more than one ending. Read a short story, then stop halfway through, and complete the story yourself. Find out how many endings you can devise. Which is best and why? The story on the next page has been reputed to be the shortest science fiction story in the world.

After the last atomic war, earth was dead; nothing grew, nothing lived. The last man sat alone in a room. There was a knock on the door ....

Can you continue and complete the story?

Poetry pieces

From an anthology or poetry books write lines or fragments from different poems on slips of paper (a pair or group can combine their efforts). Select at random some slips of paper. Read the fragments of poetry. Try to visualise what they are about. Try to compose a poem (or piece of prose) using one or more pieces of poetry and your own words.

Hear this

Shut your eyes while you listen to a new piece of music. What picture(s) come into your mind? What words come into your mind? What title would you give the music? What does it make you feel or think?

Sentence making

Choose four or five different initial letters, for example, W C E N. How many sentences can you generate using these four letters? for example: We can eat nuts. Alternatively, choose five letters, for example, E G B D F. This is a test of verbal fluency.

Common problems

What problems might arise in – taking a bath, getting up in the morning, cooking a meal, going to school or work, watching television, playing with friends, buying shoes etc.? Share problems, suggest solutions.

Improvements

How could you improve, for example, a door, a desk, the human body, school, law and order etc.

Create a character

Choose a person you would like to be. What is your name? What do you look like? Where do you live? What do you do? What are your likes and dislikes? What is your story?

Summary

Children can be helped to gain more from any learning situation if self-expression and creativity are encouraged. One of the defining characteristics of creativity is the ability to generate and explore alternatives. In practice this means encouraging a divergent range of responses, to allow for individual patterns and styles of learning. Creativity is not directly related to intelligence, but is a separate set of skills – including visual and verbal skills – that can be developed and, to some extent, assessed. A number of creative thinking techniques and teaching strategies, have been found helpful in developing divergent thinking. A creative interplay of ideas can enhance the child's capacity to learn by extending perception, helping the child see more in any given situation.[8]

References

1   Piaget, J. (1948/1974) *To Understand is to Invent: The Future of Education*, Viking, New York.

2   A useful book on the theory and practice of creative thinking is: Amabile, T. M. (1983) *The Social Psychology of Creativity*, Springer-Verlag, New York.

3   Wallach, M. A. and Kogan, N. (1965) *Modes of Thinking in Young Children*, Holt, Rinehart & Winston, London.

4   Torrance has been a leading researcher into ways of developing and assessing creativity. His books include: Torrance, E. P. (1962) *Guiding Creative Talent*, Prentice Hall; (1965) *Rewarding Creative Behaviour*, Prentice Hall, Englewood Cliffs, New Jersey.

5   de Bono, E. (1987) *CoRT Thinking Programme*, Science Research Associates, Henley.

6   von Oech, Roger (1983) *A Whack on the Side of the Head*, Warner Books; (1987) *A Kick in the Seat of the Pants*, HarperCollins, London.

7   Gordon, W. J. J. (1961) *Synectics*, Harper & Row, London.

8   For more on creative thinking see Fisher, R. (1990) *Teaching Children to Think*, Simon & Schuster, Hemel Hempstead, pp. 29–65.

7 Co-operative learning

Learning together can develop social and cognitive skills

What a child can do in co-operation today, he will be able to do alone tomorrow.
  Vygotsky (1962)

I used to hate working with other people. Now I've worked in groups, I only hate working with some other people.
  Child, aged eight

Wayne was struggling with his reading. A rather quiet and withdrawn eight-year old, he was finding it very difficult to progress beyond the most basic of reading books. He was the least able reader in his class, and his teacher was worried. A new idea had been tried in a local school. It was called peer tutoring, which meant that children worked in a structured way with a more able partner. So Wayne was paired with an older fluent reader – and they read together for fifteen minutes a day for a term. 'At first', said his teacher, 'there didn't seem to be much progress, but by the end of the term Wayne had really taken off.' Wayne put it down, not to his teacher, but to his 'reading friend'. He had learnt about reading and also something of the value of co-operative learning.

Every child is different. Even asking a simple question like: 'What are clouds made of?' will elicit a range of responses from a group of children. Each child has their own store of knowledge, ideas and experiences that she or he uses to make sense of the world. Each child has unique abilities and a learning style all their own. Should the child then be best viewed as an individual learner, as an 'active scientist' exploring the world and developing increasingly complex structures of individual thought? If all learners are individuals should all learning be individualised learning?

In the 1960s, there was a big movement towards individualised learning. It was called programmed learning and had a simple rationale: every child is individual and each has different needs, so each requires an individual programme to work through. Machines were devised and boxes of workcards and workbooks produced to allow each child to interact with the programme in his or her own way. Some good programmes were written, and they produced efficient learning outcomes. But these programmes became less effective with continued use, if they were not mediated by a teacher. Many of the materials simply invited 'busyness', for example, completing blanks in given sentences. The work was often repetitive and superficial, with little evidence of learning or thinking. The decisive influence on the success of such programmes was not the machine or the materials, but the mediating influence of another human being. Learning can be an unassisted activity. A child is given a load of bricks, a student presented with a problem, an adult given a recipe or set of instructions, and each one can respond to and relish an individual learning situation. But most learning takes place in a social context – as Bruner says: 'Making sense is a social process'.[1] For Vygotsky, social interaction has a central role in a child's education.[2] It is through being with 'knowledgeable others' that a child's potential for learning is revealed. These knowledgeable others can be anybody – parents, siblings, friends, peers, teachers or other adults. Parents are usually the primary caretakers, but anyone can act as a caretaker of a child's learning.

Much of our learning is founded on co-operatively achieved success. With others, we can do more and achieve more than we can do on our own. The reason why human beings are, at present, the most successful of the animal species is that we are able to combine the flexibility and experimental brilliance of individuals with the generative power of co-operative effort. Children learn best when they have access to the generative power of those around them. As one child said: 'I like working with others, they help you see what you are thinking.'

The basis of success-through-others is language and communication. It is through effective communication – 'co-operative talking' – that great institutions, social organisations and small task groups achieve success. We need to look therefore at two closely linked areas:

- co-operative talking *organising experience into thought with others*
- co-operative learning *learning with others, in pairs, in small and in large groups.*

The best conditions for learning exist when children have a challenge that extends their cognitive range. We help most when we encourage the child's reach to exceed its grasp. Too great a challenge risks ending in failure and frustration. Too little challenge and a child's potential will never be realised. For Vygotsky this potential – what he calls the Zone of Proximal Development – exists not just in the child's mind. It lies as much in the 'social plane', in the skills, ideas and experiences of the social context in which she or he and her or his peers inhabit, as in the 'psychological plane' or internal functions of the mind. On this view the role of the teacher is to provide the social and cognitive framework for learning, so that attention is drawn to the cognitive challenge of the task, and support is made available to meet that challenge.

The communicative framework for learning

Success in learning depends on creating a communicative framework for learning. Elements of a shared understanding can be summed up in two questions.

- Where are you? *What is the present situation, task or problem? What do you know and what do you need to know? Who and what is involved? Why is it as it is?*
- Where do you wish to be? *Where do you wish to get to? What do you want*

to do? What obstacles are in the way? How will you get there? Who or what will help? Which are the ways to go? How will you know when you are there?

Children need cognitive climbing frames to 'scaffold' their thinking that support where they are, and help them to higher levels of explanation and activity. The communicative framework should help children to:

- communicate what is known, and then
- develop new understandings through thinking aloud, grappling with ideas and clarifying thoughts, and then
- reflect on what has been achieved through thinking about what they have learnt and exchanging ideas with other students and adults.

Good teaching will help children focus not only on the content of what they are doing, but also on the processes and outcomes of their activity. Teaching is less successful, as schools inspectors' (HMIs) reports show indicate, when teachers are unclear about what they want children to learn, when tasks are not matched to children's ability, and when learning outcomes are not assessed. Simply giving children tasks, even if the content is relevant, is not enough. To help children in learning how to learn, we must try to communicate these key elements.

- Think what you intend to do and discuss what you hope to achieve.
- Think why you are doing it and express in your own words the purpose of the activity.
- Think how you are doing it and what can help you to achieve success.
- Think what you have done and reflect on the outcome (the product and the process).
- Think what you do next and how to use what you have learnt.

The Plowden Report[3] spoke of the 'twin pitfalls of demanding too much and expecting too little', but often we need to demand a little too much if we are to help children to have high expectations of themselves and to focus on the next stage in their learning, while at the same time valuing what they have achieved. It is one of the 'push me/pull you' dilemmas of teaching to maintain the right balance of high but realistic expectation. One justification of co-operative work is that we are able to expect more from children who are working together than when working on their own. But what form should this co-operation take?

Learning in pairs

Make your friends your teachers and mingle the pleasures of conversation with the advantages of instruction.
    Gracián (1647)

Like many good ideas in education, the concept of children helping children is not new. The benefits of peer tutoring were known to the Greeks and Romans. As Comenius observed: *Qui docet, discit,* (Who teaches, learns). There is no better way to learn something well than to teach it, and to teach something is often to learn it twice.

How to be a good teacher

Teach them in stages and make sure they understand all they need to know in order to learn what you are teaching.

Teach them in the simplest form and make sure they understand ~~each~~ all that you are telling them.

Ask them if they don't understand anything and if they don't go over the part they don't understand.

Ask a few questions and check that way that they understand all you are telling them.

If they are sure of it, give them a sheet of that work and see how they cope on their own.

Figure 7.1 How to be a good teacher by Tom, aged ten

Peer tutoring is a process that can benefit:

- the tutor *the helping child*
- the tutee *the child who is helped*
- the teacher *the mediator of the learning.*

Goodlad[4] says that peer tutoring is 'humanly rewarding'. What are these rewards? Social benefits arise from creating a co-operative learning environment, in promoting a sense of common purpose and in social bonding. Gains in learning can include progress in subject areas, as well as in learning how to learn (metacognitive development).

The helping child (tutor) can benefit from taking on a nurturing role. Although they are teaching material they may have mastered, the tutor can gain intellectual benefits in different ways. Putting their skills and knowledge to some purpose will help to consolidate their knowledge, fill in gaps, find new meanings and extend their conceptual frameworks. It also helps the child to understand more about the learning process, the possible blocks to learning and how to overcome them. As one child tutor put it: 'Teaching someone is not easy. You have to remember a lot of what you've forgotten. It helps you understand what you went through at that age. Having a teacher is alright but having a friend too is better'.

For the child tutee, the benefits can be considerable. The tutee is given some extra individual attention, with regular and responsive feedback on his or her efforts. The verbal interaction with a friend is of a personal and powerful kind, if it works well. The quality of teaching by a peer tutor will rarely match that of a trained teacher. Why is this so? Good teaching involves giving help when the learner faces difficulty, but offering less help when the learner shows signs of competence. Child tutors are ready to offer help, but tend not to pull back when the learner shows signs of success. Child tutors give specific concrete suggestions, and are less likely than adults to ensure the learner understands the connections between activities. Children are not so good as adults at 'scaffolding' the learning process for others.[5] They do not have the metacognitive skills of adults, they know less about the process of learning. What they do offer is a direct help in learning, and help of a companionable kind. The tutor child can provide a model of learning, and demonstrate the required behaviour – such as reading or problem-solving in maths. The tutor can model how to learn as well as offer emotional support.

What do teachers get out of it? Peer tutoring can free teachers from some of the routine work inherent in monitoring a whole class. To foster an 'apprenticeship' approach to learning teachers will need to support both tutor and tutee, to ensure that a positive social relationship is being developed.

Paired reading

I like reading with someone because it helps me to read by myself later.
    Jane, aged eight

There has been much research[6] into the benefits of paired reading. Originally intended for use with non-professional adults to help children with a reading disability, it has been found to have beneficial effects used with non-readers, retarded readers, average and able readers. The recommended approach can be summed up as follows:

1 The tutee selects a book of interest.
2 The tutoring child, or teacher, checks that the book is within the tutee's competence, e.g. by using the 'five finger test'. (This is a simple readability check. Open the book at random, spread five fingers across it, if the tutee can read the five words the book is probably appropriate. If there is difficulty in reading more than one then the book is probably too hard. If there is a problem with one word, then try again on another page.)
3 Tutor and tutee sit physically close.
4 Tutor and tutee talk about the book before the tutee reads aloud, or they read the text together.
5 If the reader is stuck on a word, the tutoring child allows a *pause* (so the tutee can think and try guessing from the context or the initial sound of the word). The tutor then *prompts* (by giving a clue, such as the initial sound of the word).
6 Praise is a key feature of the method – praise for the child who is helped, and for the helper.

The process is simple. As Goodlad put it, all you need to decide is 'who is to teach what to whom and for what purpose, how and where, when and how often'.[7] Success in this kind of learning is made up of many small steps. The recipe is – keep it short, simple and sustained. The tutoring child (or adult) needs training, for example, in the 'pause, prompt, praise' method, and the process needs to be monitored so that there is a good 'match' and positive feelings between the partners.

Paired writing

For any writer, having a 'response friend' to share the first draft of a piece of writing can be useful in providing an audience for the work, as well as in proofreading for errors and improvements in style. But children need guidance, both on how to be a good writer and how to be a good response friend. Children find it helpful to have this information made explicit. As one nine-year old said: 'You can't make it better until you know how'. This know-how needs to be put into words, for it is not self-evident. The advice one teacher has posted in her classroom on being a good writer and on being a good response friend is set out in Figure 7.2.

In learning how to learn, children need opportunities to teach, and opportunities to learn from each other. They can benefit from learning to learn in three kinds of partnership:

• equal partners in terms of age and ability as response partners to share thinking work and problem-solving
• tutor partners, who are more able, such as older students or adults who can act as 'expert' helpers
• tutee partners who are less able and can be tutored in specific learning tasks, giving the child experience of being in the 'expert' tutoring mode.

Being a good writer	Being a good 'response friend'
1 Draft your writing	1 Read your friend's work, or listen carefully as your friend reads it
2 Read it aloud to yourself	2 Tell you friend at least two good things you liked about the writing
3 Think .... Do you want to add or change anything?	3 Think how they might improve their writing. Is there anything missing?
4 Read or show your writing to someone. Is there a good beginning and ending?	4 Can you help your friend make it better?
5 Listen to what they say. Is there a way of making it better?	
6 Can you make it even better?	

Figure 7.2 Being a good writer and a good response friend

Think-pair-share

One co-operative learning strategy found useful in all kinds of learning sit-uations is summed up in the slogan: 'Think-pair-share'. Often teachers use a 'one response' strategy, meaning that one child responds in the class at a time. Think-pair-share are listed below.

1 Students listen while teacher or another poses the question or problem.
2 Students are given time to think of a response.
3 Students then pair with a neighbour to discuss their response.
4 Finally students share their responses with the whole group.

The following are some activities that can encourage paired learning:

- paired drawing *one partner draws a picture and describes the hidden picture to the other who tries to draw it from the description*
- mirror movement *one child creates a sequence of body movements for the partner to try to follow at the same time*
- shared reading *partners prepare a text, e.g. news item, story or poem, for read ing aloud between themselves or to others*
- cartoons *partners brainstorm ideas, one child draws, the other supplies captions*

- instructions *partners work out instructions, rules and strategies for doing something, e.g. playing a game or making a model, then showing others*
- paired stories *partners create a story together to retell to others*
- paired assessment *partners report on each other's work, picking out at least two good things about it and one thing to improve.*

> **TASK 33**
>
> **Peer tutoring**
> Think of a child who needs help in some aspect of learning.
> 1   Who could be a learning partner for that child?
> 2   What advice will the learning partners need?
> 3   Where should they meet? When, and how often?
> 4   In what ways can you support the partnership?
> Working with partners should also give a child confidence to work in bigger groups.

Learning in a group

I like working in a group when you know what you have to do ... when you each have a job. Otherwise you might just as well be on your own.
   James, aged eight

If all teaching were done on an individual basis, a teacher could only spend a small amount of time with each individual. More time can be spent with children when they are grouped together, and they can learn more from working with each other.

The advantages of working in a group can include the development of:

- social skills (interpersonal intelligence) *involved in working with and communicating to each other*
- cognitive skills *through having to explain, negotiate meanings and solve problems with each other*
- emotional support *through being motivated by the enthusiasm of the group or its leading members.*

These benefits do not arise simply by sitting children together. Research studies in British classrooms show that, where children were seated in groups, most of their time was spent on individual tasks.[8] Typically children work in groups, but not as groups. Sitting in groups can positively distract children from their work. Task-related talk is not always task enhancing. Typical exchanges included: 'Where are you up to, I'm on ...' 'Can I borrow your rubber? 'Do you have to underline?' Nor do children in groups necessarily get much teacher attention related to their learning. A lot of teacher time can be taken up in managing the group and organising resources. Children may also be left unsure about how much co-operation is allowed. When the teacher is present, group activity is high, but it usually drops to around 50 per cent when the teacher is not actively engaged with the group. So what should be done?

One implication of these findings is that teachers should think carefully about the purpose of grouping children. Often there are no good grounds for sitting children in groups – they would work better on individual or paired tasks, sitting individually or in pairs. It may be relevant to have different groupings for different tasks. Children will need to sit in groups for genuinely co-operative groupwork. But what is genuinely co-operative groupwork, and how is it achieved?

Grouping children together is only justified if it helps to promote more effective learning, and results in co-operative activity that extends what the individual could do alone.

Three kinds of learning in groups

1 Children working together on individual tasks.
2 Children working in a group on a task with a joint outcome, such as a problem-solving or construction task.
3 Children working together on activities which contribute to a joint outcome, e.g. chapters of a story, or research task.

The composition of groups

How should groups be composed? Do children learn better in groups of similar ability, or mixed ability? Research by Bennett and others indicates that groups of high ability children working together usually produced the highest degrees of understanding and performance in group work.[9] Next in level of performance came mixed ability and average ability groups with low ability groups working least well. High ability children tend to work well in whatever ability group they are put in. They work well together, and in mixed or low ability groups they often take the lead in explaining the task and organising the thinking of the group. The fear that high ability children miss out in mixed ability groups seems largely to be unfounded, if they are also given opportunities to work at optimal level with similar high ability children. They can gain by taking the 'teacher's' role in helping the group.

Tasks for groupwork

The important factor about groupwork is that it is not just a social experience, but should impose cognitive demands on the children involved. So what kinds of task are best suited for co-operative groupwork?

Activities suited to group working include:

• interpretative discussion *where groups investigate and discuss a given focus such as a picture, poem or artefact – pooling ideas, sharing experiences, or eliciting opinions to interpret or describe what they have been given. Examples include: group reading, putting things in sequence, e.g. cut-up lines of a poem, putting things in order of preference, e.g. pictures, putting things into sets, e.g. what will float or sink?*
• problem-solving tasks *where groups discuss an open-ended problem or situation, and decide between possible courses of action. Examples include: organis-*

ing a fund-raising event, solving an environmental or social problem, tackling a computer task, or preparing a group presentation
- production tasks *where groups work in teams to produce a material outcome, either by creating different prototypes and agreeing the best, as in designing a paper plane; or contributing different elements to a joint product, as in creating a newspaper; or working on one large product, as in making a paper tower.*

TASK 34

Group activities
Choose a topic or planned course of work in a curriculum area.
Design one or more co-operative group activities for groups of your children that relates to the chosen topic or subject.
Try to create group activities for each of the headings listed below.
1 Interpretative discussion
2 Problem-solving
3 Production for display

A useful distinction can be made between the two aspects of thinking that can contribute to a process of discussion – reflective thinking and active thinking (know-how). These two aspects of thinking relate also to two aspects of groupwork, getting group members to reflect on how the group

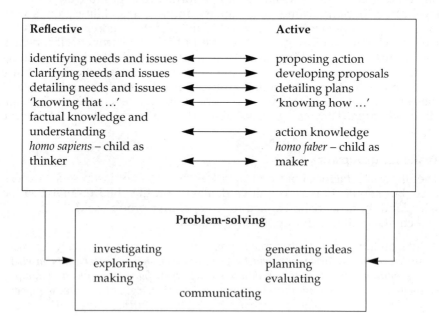

Figure 7.3 Reflective and active thinking[10]

functioned as well as on the active outcome of the group effort. Questions to ask them to discuss include:

- How well did we work as a group?
- How successful was the outcome?

Planning for groupwork

Successful groupwork depends on good planning.

In planning for groupwork good advice is to start small, start simple and start structured. One way is to give pairs of children a simple task, like predicting the end of a story. Then put two pairs together to share ideas. This is useful for each pair has a contribution to make to the discussion. The group can then share with a larger group, such as a class. This strategy can be summed up as:

Think – Pair – Group – Share

Key elements in planning for groupwork include:

- group size *which size groups work best?*
- group composition *either free choice, friendship, mixed or similar ability groups?*
- group management *what skills and strategies make for success?*

Group size

The National Curriculum asks teachers to set up different groups for different tasks and purposes. Which is the best size for groupwork? Research suggests two answers to this:

- no fixed rules *with groups of three, four or five used for different tasks and purposes*
- the rule of four *which argues that groups of four allow for maximum communication between individuals, and that in groups of three or larger than four there are often outsiders.*

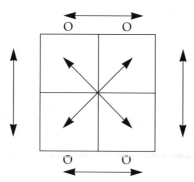

Figure 7.4 The rule of four[11]

Group composition

Two elements necessary for successful groupwork are security and challenge. Friendship groups offer students the greatest security, but not always the challenge needed to extend their thinking. Friendship groups also do not extend the social skills involved in relating to children they do not know or do not like. Success in life involves working at times with all sorts of people, and children should sometimes be persuaded to work in groups despite personal likes and dislikes. Mixed ability groups are likely to benefit the widest range of pupils, though opportunities should be given for those of similar ability, especially high attainers to work together.

Do children work better in gender or mixed-gender groups? Research findings provide no clear conclusions. Key factors seem to be the personality of individual children and the balance of skills in the group. Groups work best, irrespective of gender make-up, if they make good teams and have a blend of co-operative skills.

Groupwork skills – team building

Children need to be taught *how* to work in co-operative groups and to be made aware of the kinds of skills and behaviour that make learning in groups effective.[12] Team building is necessary to help overcome the various problems associated with working together. Skills needed include:

- the ability to understand the needs of others and to take turns
- the ability to articulate a point of view
- the ability to listen to the viewpoint of others
- the ability to respond, question, discuss, argue and reason.

These skills are not in themselves innate, they have to be learnt. They can be divided into two kinds – the cognitive skills involved in processing information, and the social skills of working as a good team member.

Various barriers may need to be overcome. Barrier behaviours include being opinionated, aggressive, over-dominating, competitive, attention-seeking, messing around, rejection of others and withdrawal. Groups will sometimes allow their 'stars' to do the work and make the decisions, and allow 'free riders' to opt out of all contributions. 'Stars', 'free riders' and other stereotypes can be identified in any group situation, staffroom or club.

The following activities help to develop groupwork skills.

Who works or plays in group teams?

Children brainstorm different kinds of groups or teams, such as sports teams, factory teams, hospital teams, school teams etc. List and share these. Choose one, for example, a sports team. Discuss: What makes for good teamwork in this team?

Who works in a group?

Brainstorm with the students the reasons for working in a group. When a teacher of six-year olds did this task the responses she received included:

- to practice getting on with one another
- to learn things other people know
- to get help with spelling
- to co-operate and help
- to listen to one another
- to think
- to solve problems
- to sort out what you will do.

What rules should there be?

Ask the children in groups to think of about six to ten rules for working together. When these have been agreed children can make a group poster to show and share with others.

Rules for discussion agreed by a group of ten-year olds
1 Give everyone a turn at speaking.
2 Don't interrupt when someone else is talking.
3 Give support and help them add things.
4 Don't say anything stupid, mean or unpleasant.
5 If people don't want to say anything they don't have to.
6 Don't laugh unkindly at something someone has said.
7 Think before you ask a question.

Can you make a group display?

Ask students to plan a display of work to which everyone in the group contributes, for example, an art mural. Try giving each member one element of the final design, for example, one colour or one shape, a writing or research project, a music or movement presentation, a design or construction, or a puppet play.

Could you survive as a group on a desert island?

Groups imagine they have been shipwrecked on a desert island. What would they need to survive? What could each member of the group offer to do to help the others survive? What tasks would need doing? How would they share these tasks?

   If they found a box washed ashore, what items would they most like to find in it to help them survive? Agree on ten items, and try to list them in order of importance. Compare lists.

Can your group give advice to help solve a problem?

Groups consider a problem that has been presented to them. They must discuss and try to agree a joint response to the problem. Examples of problems include common moral dilemmas such as: 'Two students find a five pound note in the street. What should they do with it?' or problems contributed (anonymously) by pupils themselves.

Can you read in a group?

Groups share reading aloud of a story or book, and discuss what they have read. Most students will need some guidance when asked to discuss a story, and it may be helpful to brainstorm a list of questions to help the group focus on the story, the illustrations and the way the story has been written.

TASK 35

Creating group rules
Ask groups of children to discuss, agree and write down all the rules they think will help the group to work well together.
1   Which rules do they think most important?
2   Try to put the rules in order of priority.
3   Display and discuss the rules created by different groups.

In 1811, Isaac Watts wrote:

> *If three or four persons agree to read the same book, and each brings his own remarks upon it at some set hour appointed for the conversation, and they communicate mutually their sentiments on the subject, and debate about it in a friendly manner, this practice will render the reading of any author more abundantly beneficial to every one of them.*

As anyone who has had experience of organising groupwork will know, problems are almost bound to occur. Humans are social, but not necessarily sociable, animals. Some students may be 'group refusers'. Strategies to deal with these include starting in pairs; working for short periods of time; rewarding good participation; varying the groups; allowing the child to observe a group in action; or trying firm persuasion, 'forcing the child', in Rousseau's phrase, 'to be free'. Over-quiet and over-dominating children may pose problems. Sometimes it helps to put the retiring child in a quiet group and a 'dominant' child with an extrovert group. Success in groupwork means matching children to each other and the task to the group.

Another possible problem is that group members may demand individual attention from the teacher. One way to avoid excessive demands is to have the rule: team questions only. If the child has a question, she or he must first ask a member of the team. Only the spokesperson for the team may consult with another team. If, after trying, the team cannot find an answer they may then ask the teacher the team question. The aim is to move the team from teacher-dependency to group independence. As one teacher put it: 'I'll only help them if at first they've tried to help themselves.'

Remember the old advice: 'Keep 'em busy'. Give the group a specific task to undertake, in either verbal or written form. If you have set them an open task, have an alternative or extension activity ready, such as a checklist of things to discuss or a sequencing activity. If members of the group are going to have different roles such as chairperson, scribe, reporter, expert, sort this out beforehand. Make clear to them your own role in supporting, evaluating and rewarding their group effort. The aim is of course for the group to feel, 'We did it ourselves!'

Evaluating groupwork

Evaluating the process and outcomes of groupwork is important. Students should monitor their co-operative behaviour and identify what they have learnt, and teachers or others assess should what happened during the groupwork task and its outcomes (see Figure 7.5 below).

The following questions can help children focus on different aspects of groupwork and help promote the skills of self-evaluation.

- What do you think this work was about?
- What do you feel about what happened in your group today?
- What was good about your groupwork?
- What could have made it better?
- What do you think you have learnt?

Group work: observation record

Name ....   Curriculum area ....

Date ....   Activity/Context ....

Observations

Figure 7.5   Observation record

The focus should be on what actually happened and on lessons learnt from the experience. For the teacher, the best ways of monitoring participation and progress is by a combination of:

- direct observation and note-taking (or listening to a tape-recording of group talk)
- discussion with individuals, with the group or with the class
- responses from group members, writing or drawing about the group task.

Assessment of group activity is made difficult by the complex interweaving of the social and cognitive aspects of learning. One child asked to assess what he had learned from his group activity replied: 'I haven't learnt much about building bridges but I now know how to stop Jason putting his hand up my bottom!' Many teachers are never without a notepad to record observations of students at work. It is advisable to focus on one group, or on the work of three or four children a week, trying to record key experiences and looking for the 'Aha!' moments of learning breakthrough. An example of an observation record sheet is shown in Figure 7.5.

Learning in large groups

There are many benefits to be gained from learning in large groups – the traditional approach of organising and teaching children in classes. A large group or class is a community, and should provide the benefits of community support, resources, and extended opportunities for learning. Research shows a link between successful learning in schools and high levels of effective whole-class teaching. What are the factors that make for success with children learning in large groups?[13]

Two aspects of learning in a large group

The social/cultural context

The ethos of standards and expectations created and maintained by the community, school or class can become reflected in the individual learner. A community or a school can create a powerful learning environment exerting a strong influence on the learner. A large group context can provide the essential structure, purpose and control needed for learning to flourish.

The cognitive/intellectually challenging context

The intellectual stimulus to challenge and extend the child involves the use of 'higher order questioning, explanations and statements, and these in turn correlate with higher levels of pupil performance', particularly in the basic subjects. Such teaching should aim to involve all the pupils in active thinking and responding.[14]

Not that active thinking is always seen as a good thing. As one child recently said after his class had been brainstorming for some time: 'Can't I get on by myself. All this thinking makes my brain hurt!' But another child's response was: 'I like this thinking together, 'cos it helps you think more.'

Summary

Each child is an individual and has individual learning needs. However, most human learning is a social process, with others involved in co-operative activity with the learner. Successful learning in groups requires a communicative framework. This can be achieved through co-operative work in pairs, for example, in reading or writing activities. Co-operative learning can be undertaken through discussion, problem-solving or production tasks. Considerations for effective groupwork include the activities to be undertaken and also the composition of groups and the development of groupworking skills. Children also benefit from learning in large groups. Research into co-operative learning supports the view that effective groupwork develops both the social and cognitive aspects of learning.[15]

References

1   Bruner, J. and Haste, H. (1987) *Making Sense*, Methuen, London.
2   Vygotsky, L. S. (1962) *Thought and Language*, MIT Press, Cambridge, Mass.; Vygotsky, L. S. (1978), *Mind in Society: The Development of Higher Order Processes*, Harvard University Press, Cambridge, Mass.
3   Plowden, Lady B. (1967) *Children and Their Primary Schools*, HMSO, London.
4   Goodlad, S. (1979) *Learning by Teaching: An Introduction to Tutoring*, Community Service Volunteers (CSV), London.
5   Wood, D. (1989) 'Social interaction as tutoring', in Bornstein, M. H. and Bruner, J. S. (eds) *Interaction in Human Development*, Lawrence Erlbaum Associates, Hillsdale, New Jersey.
6   Topping, K. (1988) *The Peer Tutoring Handbook*, Croom Helm, London; Topping, K. (1992) 'Co-operative Learning and Peer Tutoring: An Overview', *The Psychologist*, vol. 5, no. 4, April, pp. 151–61.
7   Goodlad, op. cit.
8   Research studies include:
Boydell, D. (1975), 'Pupil Behaviour in Junior Classrooms', *British Journal of Educational Psychology*, vol. 45, no. 2, pp. 122–9;
Galton, M., Simon, B. and Croll, P. (1980) *Inside the Primary Classroom*, Routledge, London;
Bennett, N., Desforges, C., Cockburn, A. and Wilkinson, B. (1984) *The Quality of Pupil's Learning Experiences*, Lawrence Erlbaum Associates, Hillsdale, New Jersey;
Tizard, B. et al. (1988) *Young Children at School in the Inner City*, Lawrence Erlbaum Associates, Hillsdale, New Jersey.
9   Bennett, N. (1991) 'Co-operative Learning in Classrooms: Processes and Outcomes', *Journal of Child Psychology and Psychiatry*, vol. 32, no. 4, pp. 581–94.
10   Fisher, R. and Garvey, J. (1992) *Investigating Technology*, Books 1–4, Simon & Schuster, Hemel Hempstead.
11   Fisher R. (ed.) (1987) *Problem-Solving in Primary Schools*, Blackwell/Simon & Schuster, Hemel Hempstead.
12   Slavin, R. E. (1983) *Co-operative Learning*, Methuen, London; 'A Theory of School and Classroom Organisation', in *Educational Psychologist*, Lawrence Erlbaum

Associates, New Jersey; Bennett, N. and Dunne, E. (1992) *Managing Classroom Groups*, Simon & Schuster, Hemel Hempstead.

13 Mortimore, P. et al. (1988) *School Matters: The Junior Years*, Open Books, Wells; Croll, P. and Moses, D. (1988) 'Teaching Methods and Time on Task in Junior Classrooms', *Educational Research*, vol. 30, no. 2.

14 Alexander, R., Rose, J. and Woodhead, C. (1992) *Curriculum Organisation and Classroom Practice. A discussion paper*, DES/HMSO, London.

15 In addition to the above references the following books present useful perspectives on the theory and practice of co-operative learning:

Cowie, H. and Ruddock, J. (1988) *Co-operative Groupwork: an Overview*, BP Education Service, London;

Doise, W. and Mugny, G. (1984) *The Social Development of the Intellect*, Pergamon, Oxford;

Edwards, D. and Mercer, N. (1987) *Common Knowledge: The Development of Understanding in the Classroom*, Methuen, London;

Fisher, R. (1990) *Teaching Children to Think*, Simon & Schuster, Hemel Hempstead;

Foote, H. C., Morgan, M. J. and Shute, R. H. (eds) (1990), *Children Helping Children*, Wiley, London;

Galton, M. and Williamson, J. (1992) *Group Work in the Primary Classroom*, Routledge, London;

Kagan, S. (1988) *Co-operative Learning: Resources for Teachers*, University of California, Cal.;

Kingston Friends Workshop Group (1985) *Ways and Means: An Approach to Problem-Solving*, Friends Meeting House, 78 Eden Street, Kingston, Surrey;

Reason, R. (1991) *Co-operating to Learn and Learning to Co-operate*, University College, London;

Tharp, R. G. and Gallimore, R. (1988) *Rousing Minds to Life: Teaching, Learning, and Schooling in Social Context*, Cambridge University Press, Cambridge;

Underwood, D. M. and Underwood, G. (1990) *Computers and Learning: Helping Children Acquire Thinking Skills*, Blackwell, Oxford.

8 Coaching

How cognitive coaching can assist the individual learner

In his teaching the wise man guides his students but does not pull them along; he urges them to go forward and does not suppress them; he opens the way but does not take them to the place … if his students are encouraged to think for themselves we may call the man a good teacher.
Confucius (c. 5th century BC)

The best sort of teacher is one who helps you do what you couldn't do by yourself, but doesn't do it for you.
Child, aged eight

Ask a group of people where they study best and you usually get a variety of responses – at a desk, lying on the floor, by oneself, with others, in silence, talking with others, in short bursts, for a length of time and so on. Thinking and learning is an idiosyncratic process. We all have our own unique learning style, and what works for us in one situation may not suit us in another. As Whitehead reminds us: 'Each human being is a more complex structure than any social system to which he belongs.' It is this complexity, this many-layered functioning and variability of response that makes the task of teaching and of matching levels of support to the needs of individual students so challenging. All children need support as learners, but they do not always know what support they need or where to get it. This chapter looks at some general principles of cognitive coaching, and at teaching strategies that can help children learn in a wide range of contexts.

There are occasions when students learn well both in large groups and in small groups. At some time, however, all benefit from being taught in a one-to-one situation where the teacher:

- gives individual help in learning
- shows students how to take responsibility for their own learning.

All learners need some individual interaction with a teacher, some short period of time set aside, when the teacher's attention is focused specifically on the particular needs of that individual. Research shows that this is a rare occurrence in busy classrooms, and some children – often the quiet ones who get on with their work – get by with very little individual attention. They are the 'invisible children' that exist in almost every class. If you know of a class of children, can you think who the 'invisible children' might be?

Individual children will need different kinds of help, for example, being shown a technique, given a word of advice or encouragement, or told information that will help them in their work. Cognitive coaching is giving learners a special kind of help. It is help that is generative, aimed at giving them more than knowledge in a routine fact-giving sense and in developing those open capacities that help them transfer their learning to other situations. Cognitive coaching can be summed up as teaching for transfer, seeking to teach the individual student transferable skills of learning.

Cognitive apprenticeship

Only during the 19th century did the idea arise that it might be appropriate to send all children to school for a period of time and not until the 20th century did we come to believe that all children should stay in school through adolescence, and that school came to have the prime role of preparing children for life. In previous generations, children were largely taught in family settings and through apprenticeships. Despite limitations, the apprenticeship system had some important advantages over school. It taught skills in the context of actual work. Skills did not remain abstract abilities, but were applied as knowledge in use.

One of the problems with school-learning is that it teaches skills that do not seem directly related to human purposes or the student's needs. A learner benefits not only from declarative knowledge (knowing the facts of the matter), and procedural knowledge (skills and know-how) but also *conditional knowledge*, that is knowledge about where, when and how to apply particular skills and procedures. Conditional knowledge is the kind embedded in a human context, and in the particularity of human life. For example, many studies have shown that although the 'four rules' of arithmetic (adding, subtraction, multiplication and division) are known, many students cannot see how to use them in solving simple everyday problems. Many leave school in a state of conceptual confusion about some of the basic concepts not only in mathematics, but also in science, history and other key areas of learning, for they have not learnt how to apply their knowledge. It is not surprising that schools, burdened by the demands of a heavy and abstract curriculum, can become disappointing environments for learning.

The following excerpt from a conversation with a young child reveals the roots of a lack of cognitive understanding about mathematics:

RF   Why are you working with numbers?
Child   [Working on a mathematics workbook] To colour them in.
RF   But why are you adding those numbers up?
Child   Because we have to do them.
RF   Is it a good thing to learn how to add up?
Child   Yes.
RF   Why?
Child   Because the teacher tells you to.
RF   Who else uses numbers?
Child   I don't know.
RF   Have you seen anyone else using numbers?
Child   Mary.

RF   What does Mary do with numbers?
Child [Pointing to a child on another table] She colours them in.

The cognitive apprenticeship approach means placing a much greater value on intellectual processes than the sort of production line 'busy work', such as colouring in numbers in workbooks, that is a characteristic of some classes. It introduces into school many of the features that made traditional apprenticeships effective, by encouraging students to be engaged in the kind of disciplined and productive mental work that, in the past, was applied to craft activities. Three key elements in the effective teaching of apprenticeship are challenge, context and coaching. Cognitive apprenticeship works best when students are engaged on:

- challenging tasks, that require mental effort, such as reading a text that takes some effort to understand, writing to persuade an audience, or investigating a mathematical or scientific problem which encourages students to think for themselves
- contextualised tasks, that have a purpose, such as writing for an interested audience, reading for information, or applying mathematical or scientific knowledge to real-world problems
- coached tasks, that aim to assist learning, such as observing others do what they will be expected to learn, seeing models of effective performance, and being shown standards by which to judge their own performance.

Cognitive coaching need not be time-consuming. Work with one child might take two to three minutes but, if it is based on the principles of cognitive coaching, it will have contributed to learning, and the child's ability to learn. The ideal is to make cognitive coaching a flexible part of the daily routine. A concern for all teachers is: 'How can I find time to work with one child in a room with more than 20 children needing my attention?' One answer is that cognitive coaching need not be a separate activity but part of the regular teaching pattern of the day. Another approach is to set aside a planned time of coaching for every individual child over a period of time, for example, once a week or fortnight. As one teacher put it: 'It means turning some of my routine teaching into "quality-time" teaching'.

Some of the models for cognitive coaching have been inspired by the ideas of Vygotsky who argued that children develop particular cognitive capacities through collaboration with expert practitioners. At first the child is a spectator of the activity of someone who is more expert (for example, teacher, parent or older sibling). The child, as a novice, takes over some of the work under supervision of the expert, and is gradually given more responsibility in the activity until eventually the child takes full responsibility for performing the task, with the expert as a supportive audience. Using this approach, children learn about the task at an assisted pace, joining in when they can. The gap between the level that the child can manage independently and the level that the child can reach with expert help, Vygotsky called 'the zone of proximal (or potential) development'. Vygotsky claimed that 'what children can do with the assistance of others might be, in some sense, even more indicative of their mental development than what they can do alone'.[1]

Research into the differences between good and poor learners reveals the following facts.

Good learners tend to:

- focus and concentrate on tasks in hand
- generate questions about their learning
- monitor and resolve problems as they occur
- translate what they are learning into verbal and visual images
- persevere when they fail at part of a task.

Poor learners tend to:

- lack the ability to focus on the task in hand
- lack a clear idea of the purpose of learning
- lack awareness of the skills needed to be successful at learning
- view learning as a passive activity which you either can or cannot do
- give up easily on learning tasks.

The aim for teachers is to devise ways in which poor learners can practise the strategies of good learners. One way is to ask children to think about what they do when engaged on a learning activity, such as reading. For example, they might reply: 'I miss out a word I don't know', 'I get a picture in my mind', 'If I don't understand it I read it again more slowly'. The teacher could then display these strategies in the classroom, so that poorer readers/learners can be made aware of the strategies used by better readers. 'Simplify — simplify', advised Thoreau, and it is by concentrating and making children aware of simple strategies that we can avoid complications and cognitive confusion.

TASK 36

Reflecting on thinking and learning
  Do your children think they are good thinkers and learners?
  What do they think makes good thinkers and learners?
  One way to find out what they think is to ask them questions.
  1 Can you draw (or give examples of) someone who is a good
     thinker/learner? Can you draw (or give examples of) someone who is not
     a good thinker/learner?
  2 Do you think you are a good thinker/learner? Why do you think so?
  3 What can help people to be good thinkers/learners? What stops some
     people being good thinkers/learners?

Research into effective ways of cognitive coaching[2] and into the problems of poor learners have found the following six strategies to be effective.

- focus and follow throughs
- reciprocal teaching

- summarising
- explaining
- modelling
- positive feedback.

Focusing and follow throughs

One of the recurrent complaints of teachers is: 'Why don't they concentrate?' The complaints of confused learners include: 'Where do you begin?' and 'What do I do now?' Strategies of coaching that aim to address these problems include focusing and follow throughs. In focusing we try to direct the student's attention to the important features of the problem or learning situation. We are not simply telling them what to look at or think about, but require them to tell us what the central focus of attention should be. Focusing and follow throughs aim to help children to take more time, to attend more closely and to hold the focus of attention sufficiently long enough to allow thinking processes to work. They are scaffolding questions in which the hidden (or spoken) message is to 'Look at it again' and 'Think about it more'.

Focusing is part of cognitive coaching when it makes a cognitive demand on the child. It makes a positive cognitive intervention by creating a double focus:

- a perceptual focus on the elements of the situation
- a conceptual demand for an articulated response.

Focusing, which encourages the selective attention of the child, needs to be followed up by challenges that will sustain attention. With young children and poor learners, attention tends to be episodic and is easily diverted from the task in hand. The aim is to sustain attention by making appropriate cognitive demands on the child. The skill in coaching is to match the cognitive demand to the ability of the child. Where there is no challenge, no mental effort, then no new learning will take place, and it will simply be a rehearsal of what is known. An able child summed this up by saying about his teacher: 'She's boring. She doesn't do anything that you don't already know'. But, if the challenge is too great and beyond the child's repertoire of skills, this will lead to frustration and a lost learning opportunity. Challenge needs therefore to be structured and sequential, moving from the simple to the complex, from the concrete to the abstract, from lower to higher levels of thinking. The demands for initial focusing should be extended by follow-through questions that sustain attention and make progressively greater demands on the child within the limits of their competence.

The following illustrate some examples of questions that can be used to make increasing demands on levels of attention and thinking:

- labelling *What is it? What is it called? What are you doing?*
- application (simple functions) *What do you do with it? What is it for?*
- memory *Have you said/done this before?*
- description *Tell me about it. What is happening? What does it look like?*

- selective perception *What else can you see? What is this part like? What is the problem?*
- refocusing perception *Find me the part ....? Where can you see? Show me where ....?*
- reasoning about perception *Why is it like that? Which is the most important part? What is missing?*
- comparative analysis *How are these parts similar? How are they different?*
- cause and effect *What has made this happen? What caused this? What will happen? What will be the effect?*
- predicting/hypothesising *What will happen next? What will happen if ...?*
- means-end relationships *What can you/I do to achieve the goal/solve the problem? What is needed? Why? How can it be done?*
- informal reasoning *How do you know? How can you be sure? What are your reasons?*
- logical relationships *If ... then ...? What are the implications?*
- assessing parts *Which parts are good? Which part is best? What would you change?*
- evaluating wholes *What do you think of it (as a whole)? How would you compare it with others? What could make it better?*[3]

Research into reading shows the value of helping children to re-focus, and to follow through or process information for understanding. A simple yet very important strategy is to re-read a text to gain more information and understanding of it. Other simple strategies include re-telling or summarising a story. Less able readers sometimes do not realise that re-telling is a matter of summing up rather than of repeating every part, or that you can skim, rather than re-read every word, to pick out the most important points. They are not aware that the first and last sentences of a paragraph are often particularly important in understanding what the passage is about. Other successful strategies of good readers include questioning and discussing to clarify the meanings in what they read. They also tend to predict what will come next in the text, and this adds pleasure and expectation to reading. Younger and less able children know less about themselves, the tasks they face and the strategies they employ. One approach which aims to teach these learning strategies is called reciprocal teaching.

Reciprocal teaching

'Reciprocal teaching'[4] is the name given to an apprenticeship approach which is a kind of interactive game between the teacher and learner, in which each takes it in turns to lead in teaching the other. It follows the old principle that to teach is to learn twice, and the best way for children to learn a process is to get them to teach it. The process was initially designed to help children with reading and comprehension difficulties to practice the strategies used by successful learners. It consists of four activities:

- summarising *asking children to summarise the text or why they have learnt, encouraging them to focus on the main ideas of the passage or process, and to check their understanding of these*
- questioning *getting children to ask questions about what they have read or*

learnt, encouraging attention to main ideas and to think about their own com-
prehension of these

- clarifying *asking children to clarify any problematic areas of text or under-*
standing, requiring them to evaluate critically the current state of their under-
standing
- predicting *getting them to go beyond the text and present state of affairs to*
make inferences and to justify these from clues given in the content or structure
of the text.

These activities have a dual role; a cognitive function in asking children to
work on the comprehension of a given text or learning task, and a metacognitive function in challenging their ability to reflect on their own levels of
comprehension. The procedure is to take turns in leading the discussion
about a particular section of text or task. The teacher first models the
process by summarising, asking a question, clarifying a point and predicting what will come next. Next time round, the child takes on one or more of
these activities, where possible, and gradually expands this role. The aim is
to gradually remove assistance to the learner, encouraging the learner to
take more responsibility in the learning situation. Children with learning
difficulties find it hard to take responsibility for learning and to adopt the
role of teacher, but with experience of modelling and help in verbalising
they can undertake and practise some of the comprehension and monitoring activities of more able learners.[5]

With struggling learners it is useful to break the task down into small
steps, for example, by breaking up the text to be read into paragraphs. It is a
good idea to make the process explicit, saying what you are doing and why,
and rehearsing the process. Reciprocal teaching is useful for small group
activity because the children can model for each other the processes
involved. Introduce students to the 'language' and process of reciprocal
teaching by describing and practising each strategy. When asked how
someone becomes good at reading a child responded: 'I don't know, you
either can do it or you can't'. The goal of using strategies like modelling and
guided practice is to demystify the learning process, so that children are
given greater control rather than being baffled by classroom experiences.

Summarising

Summarising is one of the strategies of reciprocal teaching and it is a useful
coaching strategy in a wide variety of contexts. It is what we ask children to
do whenever we ask questions such as: 'What did you do in school today?'
'What did we do in the last lesson?' 'How are you going to plan your project?' Summarising is important in specific teaching contexts, such as reading.
A useful rule of thumb, in assessing reading, is that if a reader cannot summarise a text it is too hard, or it needs to be re-read. Woody Allen tells the
story of when, having taken a speed-reading course, he read Tolstoy's *War
and Peace* and was asked what it was about. He replied: 'It's about Russia.'

Summarising is an excellent means of synthesising the meaning of a complex message. It is useful as a process of review, and as a prelude to evaluation. The ability to provide a good summary is an advanced, higher order

skill. It involves a number of important cognitive processes[6] including:

- judging which ideas are important
- applying rules for condensing information
- practising the communication of key ideas.

Summarising can be done as spoken or written summary, and older children should gain experience of both. The practice of taking notes and concept mapping can help in this process. As these are advanced skills, plenty of guided practice is needed. Students will need to be shown what to do and told the strategies that will help them, such as:

- deleting unnecessary material
- grouping parts into larger concepts
- picking out key terms, phrases or sentences
- creating new sentences that summarise the important points.

Children should be encouraged to 'look for the big ideas' in all that they learn. A good way to begin is for the teacher to model the process, and for the teacher to think aloud while searching for the main ideas. The following are some activities to help in developing the skills of summarising.

TASK 37

Summarising

These activities are for the teacher to model, and then for students to try.

1 Read a passage from a chosen book and summarise its main idea.
2 Retell a chosen story (such as a popular fairy tale), in the shortest number of words.
3 Write a chosen story as a short newspaper report.
  Try editing it down to 40 words, then down to 20 words.

The teacher or coach has structures of understanding that are not available to the pupil. Cognitive structures are the thinking frames through which we regulate our lives and the lives of others. One of the problems children face when entering school is to get into the thinking frames of school life. Every task that children face has its own set of thinking frames. Often these frames are implicit, like the rules of a game. For example, for cooking, the thinking frames might include knowledge of foodstuffs, use of cooking utensils, rules of safety and procedures appropriate for particular recipes. As one child, trying to remember all the rules during a cookery session, said: 'What I'm learning in cooking is how to boil my brains!' For novices, it takes mental effort to bring thinking frames to mind, to form them into the right sets and patterns, and to apply them appropriately. Without cognitive structure, the child's response to the world becomes random and haphazard.

Some cognitive structures are universal, such as the constants of time and space. Some structures are general, in that they apply to a wide range of experiences. Proverbs function as one way in which social experience is generalised. Some structures function as specific instructions, such as the cognitive structure for writing – full stop, then capital letter. These structures help children to organise their ideas, and apply them as rules in like instances. They begin as rules or recipes and gradually become internalised as automatic procedures. Other kinds of thinking frame help to structure cognitive activity. They are not so much instructions or explanations as calls to action, such as: 'In every story try to find the main idea'.

Most researchers make a distinction between these two types of cognitive structure:[7]

- structures of explanation *every story has a main idea*
- structures for cognitive activity *always try to find the main idea.*

Both kinds of structure are important. Coaching that relies only on one type of structure, for example, content instruction or process activity may be missing an important element of learning. Theory and practice, explanation and activity, structure and process are united in the informed action that is the hallmark of effective learning. This book has discussed various general strategies of cognitive activity that promote learning. These are structures that promote cognitive activity. Equally important are the structures of explanation. Good teaching can be seen as a combination or blending of effective explanation linked to cognitive activity. What is effective explanation?

Explaining

Every day millions of people coach others through explanation. Effective explanation has certain characteristics in common whether it is a policeman giving directions to a tourist, a garage mechanic explaining what is wrong with a car engine, or a mother warning her children about strangers. Some people get it right by getting to the heart of the matter, using the right words, giving appropriate examples at just the right level of understanding. Other explanations only serve to confuse, and offer no structure that we can comprehend. What are the characteristics of effective explanation? The following are some of the features identified in research.[8]

Clear structure

In every situation there are certain key elements or central ideas. The distinct nature of these concepts needs to be made clear. Aid the clarity and comprehensibility of your explanation by:

- remembering the 'rule of three' *Three linked ideas are a powerful combination. 'There are three things I want you to remember …'*
- repeating key phrases *Remember the old advice – say what you are going to say, say it and say what you have said.*
- reviewing the links between the main ideas *Link a clear opening with a closing review (which can be a summary by teacher or pupil).*

Clear language

Before giving an important speech the invited speaker was passed a card by his wife. On it she had simply written the word KISS. Afterwards he said to his wife how charmed he had been by her loving note. 'Loving nothing,' she said: 'It stood for "Keep it simple stupid".' Keep the language simple, and the children are more likely to understand the message.

Variety in presentation

Maintain interest by use of varied voice, gesture and focus of attention. Avoid monotony or too much variety of approach. In explaining to a group, try to cater for different learning styles – the audiles who like to listen, to question and to be given narrative examples (such as an illustrative anecdote); the visiles who like visual stimulus and the kinaesthetic who like practical activities.

Fluency

Pacing is important. Clarity is maintained by flow, and fluency by maintaining momentum. One way to keep the momentum going is to communicate enthusiasm and a genuine interest in the topic. As one child put it: 'I like my teacher she never stops'.

These features can be summed up as instructional clarity.[9] Teacher clarity is consistently associated with student achievement, and is one of the behaviours most often identified by students listing the characteristics of their most effective teachers. Some examples are listed below.

- She takes time to explain things, so you always understand what you have to do.
- She always asks if there are any questions, and goes over things.
- He puts it into words you can understand.

According to George Washington: 'Actions, not words, are the true criteria.' Sometimes students find it hard to act on the most patient and careful of explanations. They come to understand better by being shown by someone more able than themselves than by being told. Actions sometimes speak louder and tell us more than words.

Modelling

Teacher	Why do you think Robert Frost repeated the last line of this verse?
Student	[No response]
Teacher	[After a long pause] Well, what feelings did you have as you read the poem?
Student	Why don't you just tell us the answer?[10]

Students often resist the invitation to think for themselves. It is easier for them to be told than to think. How do we convey that the goal of learning is think for oneself? A powerful strategy for assisting learning is becoming an example or model of the process you are teaching.

Imitation is probably the chief means of learning new behaviour. Indeed it is so strong that one of the problems of maturity is developing the ability to resist imitating others. Children are socialised largely through imitating the unconscious acts of others. Traditional cultures were largely handed down through modelling rather than verbal explanation. In modern times, research into modelling shows that children acquire much of their behaviour, habits, values and many of their thinking frames, not from direct instruction but through imitating adult and peer models.[11] Modelling, to be effective, requires more than simple mimicry. Modelling needs to be structured for understanding so that it can be transformed into images and verbal guides to subsequent performance. No amount of looking at a chess master or great painter will necessarily help in your own performance of these tasks. However, if we are able to actively code the components of behaviour through watching others, then we can be helped to learn and retain complex skills.

Modelling involves performing an action or series of actions that can be processed in the learner's mind. It is an important means of assisting performance, for it is often difficult to convey in words all the information that can be included in a visual or live demonstration. Learners whose conceptual and verbal skills are underdeveloped often benefit more from physical demonstration than from verbal explanation as a means of showing learning in action.

Extended contact with a child gives a teacher opportunities to become a significant and influential model in that child's life. If emulation of others is a basic way of learning, then exhibiting desired kinds of behaviour can be a strong influence on students. This example can be shown in two aspects of modelling. The first is in the general 'teaching for thinking' behaviours that infuse all areas of the curriculum. Some examples of such behaviours are listed below.

- If listening to one another is valued, the teacher listens actively and with full attention to students.
- If taking time to think is valued, the teacher must take time to wait and think about problems or the answers of students.
- If allowing other points of view is important, the teacher must invite, consider and value different points of view.
- If 'thinking things through' is important, the teacher should model 'thinking aloud' when working on tasks or problems.
- If curiosity and questioning are of value, the teacher must share their enthusiasm for discovery and their wonder at the world.

Modelling has also been found to be effective in supporting specific areas of the curriculum. The teacher of reading, who wishes to give value to the practice of reading, will model the reading process, not only by sharing in the child's experience of books but also by showing that she or he reads books for enjoyment and information. Many teachers have a regular quiet reading time in class, sometimes called USSR – Uninterrupted Sustained Silent Reading – or ERIC – Everyone Reading in Class – in which the children *and* the teacher read books of their own choice. As one teacher says: 'If reading is important I want to show my children the pleasure and value I get out of it. We all become part of the same reading club.' Novice readers are encouraged to join in the process at a level they can manage, and which includes some experience of reading performance at a higher level. By behaving in many ways as if the desired levels of knowledge and skill were actual, novices are treated as if they are competent in the processes they engage in. In so doing, they move towards full participation in the community of readers.

Whatever the subject matter of teaching, whether mathematics, science, music, art or social studies, we can invite children into that particular club by showing how we, at an adult level, participate in those activities at our own level. Apprenticeship learning is made more powerful when we make explicit the rules of thought and relate them to the kinds of task we are engaged in. Having identified the thinking skill or process we can teach it by:

- introducing the skill *for example, how to find something in an index*
- explaining the skill *saying why the information is important*
- modelling the skill *showing how you do it*
- reviewing what was done *ask them to tell you what you did*
- reflecting on the use *where else the skill can be applied.*

Teachers of skills from physical education to art have long used demonstration as a primary mode of teaching. These demonstrations are given added value when linked to the 'thinking skills' that make for successful performance and appraisal.[12] The best kind of modelling is when teachers take on the role of intelligent novices. They model performance at a slightly higher, more coherent and informed level than is characteristic of their children. To do this, it is helpful to focus on a particular cognitive strategy and provide a model to assist the children in using that strategy. For example, a teacher wanting children to refer to evidence in an information book modelled the following 'think alouds' as she made a systematic search of the book:

> *I am trying to find out something about Henry VIII's wives. I am looking in the contents page and seeing if I can see anything – I can't see a chapter on Henry VIII's wives – but I'm not going to give up, I'm going to look up the index – it's at the back, it's alphabetical so I look down the list until I get to Henry – doesn't seem to mention his wives – so I'm going to search through the pages (turns pages) – Ah, here's a picture of someone who may be his wife – let's look at the caption – Anne Boleyn – can we find that name on the page?*

TASK 38

Modelling

Practise role modelling in a chosen subject area
Use the opportunity to share with children something you are currently learning from your own adult experience.
Share any pleasures or problems that arise, expressing these at their level of understanding.
The following outlines one way of doing this.

1 Choose a book for information or pleasure that you enjoy reading.
2 Find time to read this during a time when your children are also reading their chosen books.
3 After the reading session tell the children about your book, how you came to choose it and what you have learnt or enjoyed about it.
4 Invite questions about your book.
5 Ask the children to show and tell about their books.

When children live with criticism,
They learn to condemn.

When children live with hostility,
They learn to fight.

When children live with ridicule,
They learn to be shy.

When children live with shame,
They learn to feel guilty.

When children live with tolerance,
They learn to be patient.

When children live with encouragement,
They learn confidence.

When children live with security,
They learn to have faith.

When children live with fairness,
They learn justice.

When children live with praise,
They learn to appreciate.

When children live with approval,
They learn to like themselves.

When children live with acceptance and friendship,
They learn to find love in the world.

Figure 8.1 Children live what they learn

Positive feedback

I like what you have done. Do you know why?
Teacher to child

We all welcome praise when we feel it is honestly given and is deserved. Research studies have shown that teachers tend to blame more than they praise, and notice faults more readily than they do virtues. Effort thrives on praise. Children need feedback on their past efforts and feedforward to help them identify what will make for future success and further praise.

Feeding back on performance is a powerful means of assisting learning. Thanks to research we are now in a good position to identify the features that make for effective feedback. Feedback can take many forms, such as teacher response, test data, self-assessment, but, to be effective, it must be guided by criteria of judgement, consistency of application and proximity of response to performance. The problem with feedback in the classroom is that it can often be inconsistent or too remote to be useful. Feedback is a term derived from cybernetics, the study of information systems. It does not refer to random information travelling along unconnected lines. For information to be feedback it implies the existence of a closed loop that includes criteria by which performance can be judged against standards. It is important therefore to be explicit about the criteria being used and the standards that are being aimed for. How are these standards to be set?

One way of providing standards is to offer models. The teacher can, for example, offer a model of good performance, or students can see and study good models achieved by other students. One teacher, for example, will often show her children, as a prelude to their activity, an example of a child's work – without saying whether it is a good or bad example. The work may be a piece of writing in a writing lesson, art-work in an art lesson or way of tackling a problem in a mathematics lesson. She will then ask children to judge (provide feedback) on the work, for example, by saying: 'Can you find two good things about this ... (piece of work)?' and 'Can you say one way in which it can be improved?'

The process of feedback can be summed up in these stages.

- Children should not feel that success is too easy, or too difficult, to achieve.
- They should know what standards to aim at, and the criteria by which they should judge their own work and the work of others.
- Praise of children's work should be specific and relate to both process and performance, for example: 'I like the way you tried different methods to find the answer, and well done for getting the right answer.'

When Confucius was told that Chi Wen Tzu used to think thrice before acting, he replied: 'Twice is enough.' To optimise challenge and avoid frustration there must be feedback and review of performance. Feedback allows the chance to correct errors, and also to motivate students by giving them a sense of success, and reassurance that they are building on competent work. Forms of feedback, include verbal praise, awards and rewards. The best forms of motivation are intrinsic, and stem from the child's own belief in what they do. The most potent forms of feedback give learners a justified belief in themselves, in their capacity to learn and to review their own progress.

The good coach is like the wise ruler described in the ancient Chinese text *Tao Teh Ching*.

> *The wisest rulers the people do not notice,*
> *the next best they cherish and praise,*
> *the next best they fear,*
> *and the next best they revile.*
> *For if trust is found lacking,*
> *trust is not given.*
> *The wise ruler treasures his words,*
> *the people say: 'We did it ourselves!'*

Summary

Coaching refers to a range of strategies used to assist learning and to counter the conceptual confusions of learners. Coaching aims to create the conditions of cognitive apprenticeship, which include providing optimal challenge, purposeful contexts and assistance in performance of learning tasks. Ways of assisting performance include focus and follow-through questions, reciprocal teaching, summarising, explaining, modelling and positive feedback. Success in coaching does not depend on any one method, but a range of approaches that unite curriculum and cognitive aims, and meet the different needs and learning styles of students. The ultimate aim of the coach is to create independent learners who have the capacity to coach themselves and others.

References

1   A useful book which sums up research into various aspects of cognitive coaching is: Costa, A. L. (ed.) (1991) *Developing Minds: A Resource Book for Teaching Thinking*, ASCD, Alexandra, Virginia.

2   Meadows, S. and Cashdan, M. (1988) *Helping Children Learn: Contributions to a Cognitive Curriculum*, David Fulton, London.

3   Vygotsky, L. (1978) *Mind in Society*, Harvard University Press, Cambridge, Mass., p. 85.

4   Palincsar, A. and Brown, A. (1984) 'Reciprocal Teaching of Comprehension-Fostering and Comprehension-Monitoring Activities', *Cognition and Instruction*, vol. 1, no. 2, pp. 117–75.

5   For a discussion of reciprocal teaching and other metalinguistic strategies for developing reading skills see: Wray, D. (1994) *Literacy and Awareness*, UKRA/Hodder, London.

6   For a useful discussion of summarising, and other metacognitive strategies that aid reading comprehension see: Garner, R. (1987) *Metacognition and Reading Comprehension*, Ablex, Norwood, New Jersey.

7   For more on research into cognitive structuring see: Tharp, R. and Gallimore, R.

(1988) *Rousing Minds to Life*, Cambridge University Press, Cambridge, pp. 63 ff.

8   Gage, N. L. (1968) *Explorations of the Teacher's Effectiveness in Explaining*, Stanford University, Stanford, Connecticut.

9   Wragg, E. C. and Brown, G. (1993) *Explaining*, Routledge, London.

10   Wasserman, S. (1978) *Put Some Thinking in Your Classroom*, Benefic Press, New York.

11   Bandura, A. (1977) *Social Learning Theory*, Prentice Hall, Englewood Cliffs, New. Jersey.

12   Examples of curriculum materials which aim for cognitively assisted performance :

Fisher, R. (1994) *Active Art*, Simon & Schuster, Hemel Hempstead;

Fisher, R. and Alldridge, A. (1994) *Active PE*, Simon & Schuster, Hemel Hempstead;

Fisher R. and Garvey, J. (1992) *Investigating Technology*, Simon & Schuster, Hemel Hempstead;

Fisher, R. and Vince, A. (1989) *Investigating Maths*, Simon & Schuster, Hemel Hempstead.

9 Reviewing

A review process can enhance self-esteem and learning

A person who doubts himself is like a man who would enlist in the ranks of his enemies and bears arms against himself. He makes his failure certain by himself being the first person to be convinced of it.
  Alexandre Dumas, *The Three Musketeers*, 1844

If I think I can do something I can usually do it. When I don't think I can do it I usually fail.
  Child, aged twelve

One day an English class was asked to do something surprising. They had been given a number of co-operative tasks to undertake in small groups. These included listing as many things present in the room as they could in one minute, identifying in their list what they thought would not appear on any other list; noting the possible uses of a paper clip; discussing famous people they would like to meet and ranking the top five; and sorting strip cartoon pictures into the right order. The lesson ended with a task that was in many ways the most challenging. The students were asked to write down what they thought they had learned from the lesson. Some of these reviews began in the following way.

- From this lesson I've learnt that you have to work in a group to achieve certain things …
- I think this lesson was quite good, it made us think of things quickly …
- I think this lesson was well worth having, because of the pleasure it brought me …[1]

What was new to the students was that they were not being treated simply as passive recipients of teaching, but were being regarded as active reviewers of their own learning. This process of review can help build self-esteem and self-awareness, and will provide a useful focus for thinking about learning.

Self-esteem

One factor in the possible success or failure of any human endeavour is that precious source of energy known as 'self-esteem.' This is true of learning as in other areas of life. If children develop a sense of inadequacy in themselves as learners, they will live self-fulfilling prophecies like 'I cannot learn …. I am not capable …. I am no good at anything'. They will grow to lack a positive sense of self-worth and self-competence. They will develop what has been called 'learned helplessness'.[2]

Children who do not have a self-image of themselves as active participants in learning will look elsewhere for sources of self-respect, such as any
aimless social activity that gives a sense of self-worth. Studies have shown
that self-esteem is not related to family, education, wealth, geographical
location, social class, father's occupation or having a mother at home. It
comes from relationships with those who play a significant role in the
child's life. It is formed by the person's assessment of the 'self-pictures'
which are daily reflected back from others.

Self-esteem is the quiet inner knowing that we are all right, that our
worth is recognised by others as well as by ourselves. It is a sense of self-
respect, a feeling of self-worth, a knowledge of who we are and what we
can do. The main sources of this feeling come from:

- affirmation of positive qualities from parents, teachers and other significant caretakers
- recognition from peers, siblings and other children
- self-belief in themselves based on their own experiences of competence
  and success.

Children value themselves as learners to the degree that they have been
valued. To focus on achievement in learning without also focusing on
building self-esteem is only to half-educate a child. Research has consistently shown a correlation between self-esteem and achievement in reading,
writing, mathematics and other subjects.[3] It is an area no teacher or parent
can afford to neglect. It is a necessary, but not a sufficient condition for success. Self-esteem by itself is not enough for it can encourage an uncritical
self-satisfaction. What is needed is to link self-esteem to self-awareness, and
to create in children what has been called 'mastery orientation'.[4]

Mastery orientation

Mastery orientation refers to a sense of self-competence or self-efficacy that
children develop from an early age and that moulds their approach to
learning. It is the attitude of: 'I am good at tasks and know how to do them'.
Children who are mastery oriented are curious, they want to learn, and
have developed the resilience to cope with failure and frustration. Mastery
orientation makes for success in learning, particularly in the ability to
respond to challenges, and to succeed in new learning tasks. Some of the
characteristics of mastery orientation and learned helplessness are set out in
Figure 9.1.

The style of 'helpless' or 'mastery' oriented behaviour is not related to
intelligence, but is a personality characteristic; a way of viewing oneself and
one's capacity to be effective with people and circumstances. All individuals, whether children or adults, fall somewhere along the continuum
between helplessness and mastery. Some children have developed the characteristics of mastery orientation or of learned helplessness by the time they
first enter school. Researchers in school entry (reception) classes, observing
four and five-year olds, have noted that some children show more mastery
orientation than others.[5] They observed, for example:

Mastery orientation	Learned helplessness
Willingness to try hard tasks	Unwilling to face challenges
Views problems as challenges	Views problems as 'tests' of ability
Accepts failure without excuses	Quick to offer excuses for failure
Flexible in approach, tries other ways	Rigid in approach, gives up easily
Is self-motivated by learning	Looks for approval in learning
Wants to achieve learning goals	Wants to look good
Has a positive view of his/her competence	Has a negative view of himself/herself
Has a positive view of learning	Has a negative view of learning

Figure 9.1 Mastery orientation and learned helplessness

- reactions to difficulty *some children avoid challenge and give up easily, whereas mastery-oriented children persist in the face of obstacles*
- independence *mastery-oriented children show themselves to be more independent and less reliant on teacher guidance*
- attitude to learning *mastery-oriented children are not afraid of new, challenging experiences, and choose learning activities such as reading books during times of free choice.*

By the age of nine, children can be seen to be developing either a mastery or helplessness orientation to learning. Some children have a much clearer idea about the aims of learning, and about their own capacities to learn than others. They are more aware of their own thinking processes and whether their skills match up to the demands of a task. These abilities are developed through giving children opportunities to review what they do, to assess what they have learnt and to draw out lessons or targets for the future. It is not sufficient that children have the self-confidence to tackle intellectually demanding tasks, they also need some objective diagnosis of strengths and weaknesses in order to pursue goals successfully.

Another element in mastery orientation is the belief that intelligence can be developed. Studies show that some children believe that effort will lead to increased intelligence. 'You can become clever if you try hard', said one six-year old. Other children believe you can either succeed in a task or you cannot, and they show little capacity for effort. As one child said when encouraged to pursue a problem-solving task: 'It's a waste of time'. Sometimes this negative view is a result of teacher criticism, sometimes of a parental belief in 'natural talent'. As one seven-year old said: 'I'm no good at numbers, neither was my Dad. He says I'm like him.' In studies of the relatively poor performance of American children in mathematics the following factors were among those cited:[6]

- insufficient time and emphasis given to academic activities
- children and parents overestimated the children's accomplishments

- children's academic achievement was not a widely shared goal
- parents showed little involvement in children's schoolwork
- parents believed that 'natural talent' was more important in success at school than hard work.

In contrast, countries such as China and Japan, where levels of mathematical achievement measured by test scores have been shown to be higher than in the USA or in Britain, one factor could be the belief of parents that intelligence is malleable, and that children can achieve educational advancement through effort. In Asian countries, there is a general view that children's effort is even more important than innate ability in determining school success. The most important legacy of this view, linked with high expectations and parental support for learning, is that these children show many of the characteristics of mastery orientation that make for a success in learning.

When researcher Michael Rutter reviewed the literature on the effects of children's education on their development, he concluded that: 'The long term educational benefits stem not from what children are specifically taught but from the effects on children's attitudes to learning, on their self-esteem, and on their task orientation.'[7] How can we encourage mastery-oriented children, and move them away from a sense of helplessness? How do we help children view the inevitably difficult problems they face in learning as challenges to be mastered through effort? How do we support both self-esteem and self-effort on tasks?

The following sections outline three ways in which teaching children to learn can help enhance self-esteem and mastery orientation. These are:

- personalised learning *relating learning to personal interests, thoughts and imagination, and encouraging a sense of personal responsibility and ownership of the learning process. At its best this is what 'child-centred' or 'student-centred' learning is trying to achieve.[8] Do my students understand how the topic they are learning is relevant to their lives?*
- reviewing achievement *identifying their areas of success and in seeing where and how they can improve in by recognising, recording and reporting achievements in learning and in efforts to learn. Do my students review their progress, effort and goals for the future?*
- self-assessment *encouraging self-regulation to increase control of the learning process, and developing insight into their thinking and learning. Do my students have opportunities for assessing their learning strategies and achievements?*

Personalised learning

I shall only ask him, and not tell him, and he shall share the enquiry with me ....
    Socrates

Personalised learning is a collaborative approach to learning in which students are encouraged to link the content of the curriculum with their own personal concerns. There are two aspects to personalised learning:

- reviewing teaching to see that it is linked to the personal concerns and goals of students
- reviewing learning so that links are made to the personal concerns and goals of students.

The following example is from a lesson on fractions in mathematics, a subject which often fails to become linked to human concerns. At the start of the lesson, the teacher tries to personalise the topic, by helping the students appreciate how the topic of fractions is relevant to their lives. The teacher 'sells' the topic, and gets the students involved by brainstorming, on the board, examples of how fractions are used in everyday life, The teacher might start by asking: 'Can you think of any examples in life where something whole is split up into parts?' Examples from one class included: dividing things into equal shares – a cake, a bar of chocolate etc.; sports matches – a game of two halves; television programmes; the school timetable; time; weights; measures; journeys; phases of the moon and so on.

An effective way to begin planning for teaching is to review the factual information and skills you want your children to learn. If, for example, you were wanting to teach about another country, you might want the children to learn about:

- the map of the country
- the place of the country in relation to other countries
- places and regions within the country
- the physical environment, weather and climate
- the ways of life of the people, where they live and how they live
- the natural resources and products of the country.

A good starting point might be to write down the key questions you would like to have the children answer about the country. The personal questions to ask ourselves might include the following.

- What do you know about the topic of study?
- What would you like to find out?

Similarly a good starting point with children is to find out what they know, for example, by asking them to write, note, map and share with others their existing knowledge. Also, to ask them what they want or need to find out – what questions have they got? The following is a personal list of questions written by a ten-year old about the proposed study of another country.

- How many people live there?
- What languages do they speak?
- Is it a clean country?
- How many different kinds of transport are there?
- Is it mainly countryside or city?
- Is it a rich or poor country?
- What is their national anthem?
- Is it densely populated or not?
- Do they have many endangered animals there or not?
- Do they have a good government?

The child has here a number of useful questions for research – more power-ful because they are personal questions that she or he wants to find out – as well as some means for assessing at the end of the study what *has* been found out. What answers, after studying the topic, would the child now give to these questions – What questions have arisen during the study that she or he would like answering? How could she or he set about finding the answers? What questions have others asked? What might be the answers?

In personalising the curriculum and expecting children to take some responsibility for their own learning, we want them to relate to what they are learning, to try to involve their personal interests, thoughts and imagi-nation. One way that has proved effective is to ask 'you-questions' which aim to help the student identify with the subject matter. 'You-questions' are addressed directly to the student. They should be relevant to personal expe-riences, interests and feelings and invite personal opinion, knowledge and experience. They can also be discussed and shared with others. Below are listed examples of 'you-questions'.

- What do you know about it?
- What do you want to know?
- Have you ever been to ...?
- Have you ever heard about ...?
- What do you think it feels/felt like ...?

TASK 39

Reviewing personal goals
In any learning task the students can be invited to review what they want to achieve.
1 Choose a topic of study and ask students to identify the task and goals (aims) of learning.
2 Ask them also to identify the outcome(s) and to specify criteria for success. The chart below shows one way of recording a review of personal goals.

Topic ....

Task	Goal
Outcome	Criteria for success

One aspect of personalised learning is feedforward, in helping the child to set the scene, and identify future targets for learning, another is feedback in helping the child realise what she or he has learned and has achieved. The process is a continuum, and reflects 'time future contained in time past' (T. S. Eliot). Looking back, helps us to look forward. To plan for the future, we need to build on what we know of the past. To know where we are going, we need to know where we have been. We need to set targets, build on achievements, and set further targets for achievement.

Reviewing achievement

What is an achievement in learning? A group of children brainstormed their own definitions and came up with this list.[9]

An achievement is something:

- you can be really proud of
- you have never done before
- that you kept on trying to do and finally succeeded
- you have done which you found difficult
- you have worked hard to finish
- you have done what teachers tell you is good.

We tend to thrive under the sun of praise. We want to know what is special about us, what is praiseworthy. But we want the praise to be genuine and to be specific to us. Children need help in identifying their areas of success and in seeing where and how they can improve in the future. The following questions can help in this process.

- What have you learnt? *Assessing learning.*
- What have you achieved? *Assessing achievement.*
- What do you feel good about/proud of? *Assessing positive feelings.*
- What do you like doing/learning? *Assessing preferences.*
- What do you do well? *Assessing strengths.*
- What do you find hard? *Assessing difficulties and problems.*
- What don't you know/understand? *Assessing obstacles to learning.*
- What do you want to be able to do/improve/learn? *Assessing targets and plans for the future.*
- What support would help? *Assessing the need for support.*
- What do you think of yourself as a learner? *Assessing self-esteem as a learner.*

Many teachers see the value of setting aside a particular time to talk through what children are learning and have learnt. It is a review time, a learning conversation, or conference – a time to appraise and assess how the child is doing; to recognise achievements; to establish needs and show that these needs are understood; and discuss the next steps in learning by agreeing and setting targets. The aim is to build self-esteem by developing in the child confidence in themselves as learners and to give them an increasing sense of control over the learning process so that they can become more independent learners.

Finding sufficient time in which to conduct learning conversations and reviews with individual children is a major problem for many teachers. Most find it necessary to adopt a planned approach to managing review time. Ways in which this can be achieved include:

- daily reviews *setting aside five or ten minutes at the same time each day, for example, after lunch, for a review session with one or two children*
- weekly reviews *setting aside a longer session each week, e.g. one afternoon, to review progress with a group of children*
- termly reviews *setting aside a period once a term to interview each* child *about their progress and achievements, possibly linked to a parents' meeting*
- annual reviews *setting aside some time for each child to discuss the work of the year and to set targets for the coming holiday/year.*

In review sessions with children the aim is to help them become better learners. Be positive about what the child can do. Keep in mind a wide range of achievement. Achievements can be in the field of personal and social endeavour, taking responsibility, for example, for an aspect of work or activity, being able to work constructively with others, showing persistence when work is difficult and participating in a wide range of activities. Achievements in school include evidence of progress within curriculum areas, new developments in knowledge and skill, and participation in extra-curricular activities. Out-of-school achievements include the development of interests and pursuits (hobbies, collections, computer etc.), membership of clubs and organisations, social and cultural achievements (such as languages spoken), and special skills in music, sport etc. Taking part, if it involves effort, can also be an achievement.

In carrying out a review with a child, try to move from 'what' questions, such as: 'What do you think your best piece of work was?' to the much harder 'why' questions, such as: 'Why do you think your mathematics has improved?' The review should be more than a question-and-answer session, but should encourage children to speak freely and honestly about their learning experiences, and to discuss specific samples of work. As children begin to reflect on what they have done, and what has helped them, they are given the opportunity to reflect on what they could or should do in the future and what will help them achieve these goals.

Sometimes it is helpful with older children to keep a record of the review, to formalise the recording of achievements and the setting of targets. Figure 9.2 shows one way of recording a review.

Self-assessment

One of the aims of this process is to help children move from an external point of reference to an internal point of reference. For example, when one seven-year old was asked about her reading, during a review time with her teacher, she replied: 'I think I'm good at reading because you know yesterday when I was reading with Mum she said, "Well done".' However, another child had some other criteria by which to assess her reading: 'I have improved because last year I couldn't have read a book like Roald Dahl's *Witches*. I still don't know all the words but I can follow the story. I just guess them when I get stuck.'

Review

Record of a review between .... Student

and .... Teacher

on .... Date

Achievements

What things are you pleased about?

What things have you done well?

What things have you worked hard on and improved?

Who or what has helped you?

Agreed plans and targets

What are your plans for the future?

What do you want to try to achieve?

What will you try hard to improve?

What help will you need?

Signed .... Teacher .... Student

Figure 9.2 Review

TASK 40

Reviewing achievements

My school report

1 Ask your children to design a school report, e.g. leaving a space for subject title, comment and grade (or mark)as below.

Name ....

Date ....

Subject	Comment	Grade

2 Ask the children to make brief comments and award themselves grades in each area of the curriculum. Use the report as a basis for discussion about how the child sees their own progress in learning.

Reviewing work

One way of structuring a child's assessment of themselves is to give them statements to complete.

1 Tell them you want to know what they think and why they think it, e.g. ask the child to complete these four statements relating to a chosen subject or area of study, and to say why they made that assessment:

My best piece of work was ....

The work I most enjoyed was ....

What I found most difficult was ....

In the future I'd like to ....

(My targets for the future/next term/next year are ....)

The aim of these discussions is to make achievement the focus, and to keep in mind a wide range of achievements. Remember that taking part can be an achievement, for example, being a participant in learning experiences, events and activities. Self-assessments are useful for helping children discover not only what they are good at but also to help them identify areas of weakness so that they can begin to think about ways to improve. Sometimes writing about yourself is easier than talking about yourself. The following is a simple format for encouraging children's response to a task or area of learning. You may wish to encourage the child to make a fuller assessment of themselves as thinkers or learners. One way of doing this is to devise a questionnaire that asks a child to respond to a range of aspects of his/her learning (see Figure 9.3).

Self-concept as a thinker

Name .... Date ....

The following are statements to help you describe how you feel about your own thinking. There are four possible answers. Tick the one that best describes your thinking. Please answer all the questions.

		Never True	Rarely True	Mostly True	Always True
1	I am not good at thinking	....	....	....	....
2	I am lazy at thinking	....	....	....	....
3	I am good at saying what I think	....	....	....	....
4	I am good at thinking about many things	....	....	....	....
5	I often run out of ideas	....	....	....	....
6	I am good at thinking of new ideas	....	....	....	....
7	I like thinking about difficult problems	....	....	....	....
8	I find it hard to think in real life	....	....	....	....
9	I find it hard to concentrate	....	....	....	....
10	I am good at telling people my ideas	....	....	....	....
11	I get easily confused in my thinking	....	....	....	....
12	I usually know how to tackle a problem	....	....	....	....
13	I am good at asking questions	....	....	....	....
14	I think before deciding what is right	....	....	....	....
15	Other people listen to my ideas	....	....	....	....
16	Other people understand my ideas	....	....	....	....
17	I think about my thinking	....	....	....	....
18	I am not as good at thinking as my friends	....	....	....	....
19	I find it hard to remember	....	....	....	....
20	I am good at making plans	....	....	....	....
21	I don't think before I act	....	....	....	....
22	I am good at thinking things through	....	....	....	....
23	I find it hard to make decisions	....	....	....	....
24	I can work things out for myself	....	....	....	....

Figure 9.3 A questionnaire

Another aspect of student assessment is the evaluation of the teaching they receive. What did they think of the lesson? What did they learn? What do they still need to learn? Asking children to review what they learnt can be instructive for the teacher as well as for the students. Children are able to assess, in a subjective way, but informed by a long experience of teachers and teaching, any lesson or series of lessons. This review can be written or spoken. Lessons can be given a numerical mark, such as a percentage, or judged against an agreed scale, or children can write a short review in a learning log.

Review time needs to be planned. Some teachers prefer to leave time at the end of each lesson or session, others choose a weekly review time. What is important, is that criteria are discussed. What makes for a good lesson? What would help them to learn more? What should they learn next? The following task helps a child to gain a rapid feedback on any learning experience.

TASK 41

Assessing what we know

After a lesson or period of study, ask students to assess:

1 what they know (or understand)
2 what they think they know
3 what confuses them about the topic of study.

One way of recording this is, in three columns or boxes, to write what they:

(√)know or understand

(?) think they know or understand

(x) do not understand (are confused by).

A useful strategy for encouraging the articulation of doubts, problems, confusions and uncertainties is to have a problem box in which students may put 'help slips'. In one class when the children were asked to review the usefulness of their problem box, they wrote the following.

- It's a good way to get messages to the teacher.
- When we get stuck it means it can get sorted out.
- Sometimes you need help but do not know how to ask for it. Now we can use the problem box.

Problems can be tackled by the teacher, or shared with the whole class. The message of the problem box is that we all have problems. It helps to say what your problems are and that they can be solved if you ask for help.

Children can also be helped to gain self-awareness through thinking about what goes on in their minds or brains when they think and learn. The aim is to help them to become more self-aware, more conscious of their mental processes and to show them that they have some control over the way their brains work – some self-mastery. The following are some reflective comments by children on how they would describe the workings of their brain:

My brain is like a massive forest. It's full of amazing ideas. But some of these ideas are like shy animals, they hide away in the middle of the forest. I don't think we can ever really understand how our brains work.

My brain is like an anthill, with millions of tiny passageways. There is always something going on in my head. The ants in my mind never seem to rest. I just hope there aren't any ant-eaters!

My brain is like a naughty puppy. It never seems to do what I want it to. If I've got maths homework to do it wants to read a comic or watch TV. But like a puppy it can be trained.

Children can also be encouraged to draw the workings of their brains and minds.[10] Drawing is one way of organising thinking, another way is through organised talking (see Chapter 4), and another approach is thinking through writing. Writing has a key role to play in facilitating thinking and learning in all subjects. There has been much research into ways of developing the link between thinking and writing.[11] Many teachers encourage their students to keep journals, Learning-logs or Think-books as intellectual diaries in which to record their questions, observations and feelings about what has been taught, as a form of continuing review of the learning process. What arises from research into the use of student journals, is that children need help in keeping and learning from their journals. One way of helping children is to make the journal interactive, with the teacher or a chosen response partner making a written response to journal entries. Some teachers prefer to make the journals private, so that children can feel free to record their true feelings and observations – like a writer's journal. Expressing their own observations and knowledge in their own words, helps them to come to know and understand more about what they have learnt and about themselves as learners. Figure 9.4, on page 136, shows a child thinking, through writing, about the process of writing.[12]

Every child needs a personal tutor, or mediator, of their learning experience who can facilitate the processes of review and reflection. The following are some of the principles of mediated learning which Feuerstein and his team of researchers[13] have identified as essential to children's learning. The process of review is an ideal means for developing these important metacognitive functions which are the tools of independent learning:

- inner meaning *having a sense of purpose about learning, knowing the reasons for, and the value and significance of learning activities*
- self-regulation *developing the need to think about and plan your work, encouraging self-control and personal responsibility in learning*
- feelings of competence *feeling confident about learning, knowing what you can do and how to get help*
- feelings of challenge *being self-aware, knowing how to deal with challenge and difficulty*
- communicating *developing the ability to communicate, to share thoughts through discussion, writing and creative expression*
- setting targets *setting your personal goals or objectives to aim for, having high but realistic expectations*
- being aware of self-change *knowing that you can change, gaining feedback on learning and identifying achievements.*

Writing.

When I start to write a piece of writing I always build on a central idea, I prefer to work in quietness. If the piece of writing has to be good then I'm always concentrating. First of all I jot down ideas then I arrange them into the piece of writing. I then start to change words, I change non-interesting words for interesting ones. Make your work eye - catching and set it out so it looks good. Check for spelling mistakes. Never waste a good word, always try and fit it in. I like to read others work and grasp ideas from it. Look at ideas from all sides and find their best meaning and use. Use words that fit well in the piece of writing. Never stop concentrating, sometimes it helps to discuss your ideas with a friend.

John Mannaing.
11 years of age

Figure 9.4 A child thinking about writing

Summary

In helping children to review their learning, we can develop in them a more confident sense of themselves and increase their awareness of themselves and of the learning process. This means finding ways to enhance self-esteem and a sense of mastery in learning. This can be achieved through personalised learning which focuses on the needs of the learner, through recognising achievement, setting targets for learning, and through developing skills in self-assessment. The skills of self-assessment can help the student develop increased self-awareness and many of the metacognitive tools needed for independent learning.

References

1   For more on this lesson see: Richardson, R. (1990) *Daring to be a Teacher*, Trentham Books, Stoke-on-Trent, pp. 113–24.
2   For more on learned helplessness see:
    Diener, C. L. and Dweck, C. S. (1978) 'An Analysis of Learned Helplessness' (1), *Journal of Personality and Social Psychology*, vol. 36, pp. 451–62;
    Diener, C. L. and Dweck, C. S. (1980) 'An Analysis of Learned Helplessness' (2), *Journal of Personality and Social Psychology*, vol. 39, pp. 940–2.
3   For more on research into self-esteem see: Lawrence, D. (1988) *Enhancing Self-Esteem in the Classroom*, Paul Chapman, London.
4   Dweck, C. and Leggett, E. (1988) 'A Social-Cognitive Approach to Motivation and Personality', *Psychological Review*, vol. 95, no. 2, pp. 256–73.
5   Jowett, S. and Sylva, K. (1988) 'Does the Kind of Pre-School Matter?', *Educational Research*, vol. 28, pp. 21–31.
6   Stevenson, H. and Lee, S. (1990) 'Contexts of Achievement', Monographs for the *Society for Research in Child Development*, vol. 55, 1–2, Serial no. 221.
7   Rutter, M. (1985) 'Family and School Influences on Cognitive Development', *Journal of Child Psychology*, vol. 26, no. 5, pp. 683–704.
8   Brandes, D. and Ginnis, P. (1986) *A Guide to Student-Centred Learning*, Blackwell, Oxford.
9   Fisher, R. (1991) *Recording Achievement in Primary Schools*, Blackwell, Oxford; Johnson, G., Hill, B. and Tunstall, P. (1992) *Primary Records of Achievement*, Hodder, London.
10 For examples of children's drawings of the workings of their brain see: Fisher, R. (1990) *Teaching Children to Think*, Simon & Schuster, Hemel Hempstead, pp. 9–10.
11 Glatthorn, A. A. (1985) *Thinking and Writing: Essays on the Intellect*, ASCD, Alexandria, Virginia, pp. 36–57.
12 John Manwaring's writing is taken by permission from: Corbett, P. (1992) *Poetic Writing in the Primary School*, Kent Reading and Language Development Centre.
13 Feuerstein, R. (1980) *Instrumental Enrichment: An Intervention Program for Cognitive Modifiability*, Scott, Foresman & Company, Glenview, Ill.

10 Creating a learning environment

Ways to create effective communities for learning

A good school does not emerge like a prepacked frozen dinner stuck for 15 seconds in a radar range [microwave]; it develops from the slow simmering of carefully blended ingredients.
    Ted Sizer

I learn best when I'm with other people, sometimes this is in school, sometimes it isn't.
    Student, aged twelve

In a tough inner-city school in London a teacher has a class of low-achieving children, many of whom are from socially and economically deprived backgrounds. She is keen to raise a sense of self-esteem and expectations of achievement in her children. She calls them all 'Smarties' and says they are smart and sweet, smart of mind and sweet of nature (they are also of many different colours). By affirming they are smart, not once but repeatedly, she hopes they will come to believe it. She tries to 'catch them being good', good at their work and good in their response to others. She encourages them to make affirmations about each other – 'John tell us who you think has been working well in your group ....', 'Selina pick out someone who has been helpful to you today ....', 'Ricky can you find two good things to say about Sophie's story?'

What are the characteristics of a community which supports the success and achievements of individuals within it? One of the characteristics is that of 'high cohesion', which is the sense of belonging, of shared purpose and support within a group. The strength of a high-cohesion group is that it has a strong identity. Examples of these might include: a high-cohesion society (like Japan), a high-cohesion school (like Eton), or a successful sports team (like the All Blacks). A potential disadvantage of high-cohesion groups is that individual growth can become subservient to group norms, as anyone who has experienced the stifling influence that village life, or a very close-knit family, can sometimes create. The ideal is to belong both to a high-cohesion group and to one that supports the growth of each individual. The following are some elements that can support an ethos of success in learning for the group and for the individuals within it. A positive climate evolves out of:

- loyalty *nurturing a sense of belonging to a community, showing loyalty to individuals within the community and communicating confidence in the group's ability both to think and learn*

- trust *involving members in decision-making and giving each some responsibility in negotiating the outcomes of learning*
- support *offering help and encouragement in learning, being committed to the growth and learning of individuals*
- dynamism *showing energy and enthusiasm in the pursuit of goals and sustaining morale when faced with the challenges of learning*
- expectation *setting goals, being clear about assumptions, beliefs and learning outcomes*
- communication *sharing information about success and failure, and creating a common bond of shared knowledge.*

All successful supportive communities share some, or all, of the above characteristics. In good schools, these evolve over time and are the fruit of the sustained vision of the head and teachers within the school. Thus, the traditions or cultural values of the school are built up and provide a continuity of purpose through times of change and challenge. The school is made up of smaller learning communities, such as individual classes, and these can provide powerful environments for learning.

Creating a learning community in the classroom

In a sense a supportive group is like a tribe. The themes of identity, support and community – the sense of belonging, inherent and admired in traditional tribal societies – can help create a powerful environment for learning.

One successful programme for building supportive communities in the school or classroom is called 'Tribes'.[1] The Tribes Programme organises a class into groups of five or six children who work together throughout the school year. The children can name friends they wish to have in their tribes, but each tribe must have a mixture of boys and girls and be of mixed ability. The aim is to develop, in each group, positive peer regard, so that it will create a supportive climate for learning that will help enhance self-image, positive behaviour, and academic achievement.

There are certain ground rules that students are expected to honour at all times within their groups. Among the behaviours that are expected to become the norms of the group are:

- attentive listening *paying close attention to one another's words and feelings, giving care, respect and consideration*
- no put-downs *appreciating others, making helpful contributions and avoiding negative remarks, name-calling, hurtful gestures or behaviour*
- right to pass *choosing when to participate in group discussion and activity, having the right to silence within the a group setting*
- confidentiality *honouring the group's sharing, being confident that 'what we say here stays here'.*

These rules, or similar ones agreed by the groups and expressed in their words are posted in a prominent place in the classroom. What makes the Tribes process unique is the establishment of long-term support groups within the classroom, rather than the random and changing groupings found in many classrooms. It emphasises the need to get the setting for learning right and that an intentionally created support system will help create a more dynamic and supportive environment for learning. It stresses the importance of teacher and peer-role modelling to teach inter-personal skills and caring behaviour. In focusing on children's social development, it aims also to enhance academic achievement and the ability to learn.

One of the key aims of creating a learning community should be to foster a sense of inclusion in the group and in any group endeavour – to help children feel included and of value. We want them to be a part of the club of thinkers and learners. This means that three basic opportunities should be provided within any group setting or learning environment:

- introduction *each member needs to introduce himself or herself not just by name but by being given the chance to describe his or her interests and experiences*
- self-expression *each person should be able to express what she or he hopes and expects from the group's time together, a chance to be part of setting the agenda*
- acknowledgement *each person needs to be acknowledged as having been heard and appreciated.*

All learners feel, at times, vulnerable and defensive. Time spent on building a sense of inclusion and trust, is time well spent. Learning is not easy to achieve at times of emotional disturbance or social disruption. If emotional needs are ignored the energy of the learner is deflected away from his or her capacity to accomplish learning tasks. In helping children to state their feelings clearly, or to discuss and reflect on situations of concern we are helping them to learn about themselves and about other people. If we can utilise the co-operative spirit of the group to address problems and support individuals, we are creating powerful allies in the process of creating renewed energy for learning.

Circle time

An activity central to approaches which aim to build a community (see also Community of Enquiry (page 51) is 'circle time'. The usual format for this is to sit in a circle, with the teacher as part of the circle, leading the group in a sharing activity. Experience in the large group provides an opportunity to model the norms we hope the child will follow in other, smaller learning groups. The virtue of a circle is that everyone can see the face of every other member – and can talk person to person with any other member.

It is important that the teacher models the norms she or he hopes the children will learn, and in particular that most difficult of skills – attentive listening. Attentive listening means acknowledging the speaker, giving full attention and eye contact. It means that attention is given not only to the words that are spoken, but also to the feelings behind the words. As one child put it: 'What you feel is part of what you say....' We all find it easy to pretend to listen, but there are tell-tale signs. We can see in the eyes of others when they are not attending, when their thoughts are elsewhere, when the shutters are open but no one is at home.

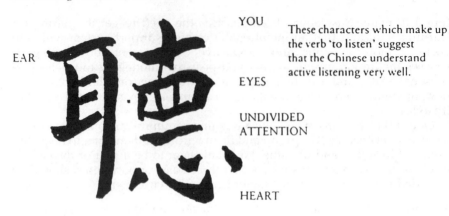

Figure 10.1 Chinese characters: 'to listen'

Some of the active listening skills that we should practise include:

- attending *listening silently with full attention*
- encouraging *through non-verbal (nodding) or verbal ('Uh huh') means*
- paraphrasing *'What I heard you say was ....'*
- responding *responding to the words, and reflecting feelings ('You sound sad ...').*

A book written many years ago with the title, *The Geranium on the Windowsill Just Died, but Teacher, You Went Right On*, was about a teacher who refused to acknowledge anything not in her lesson plan. She did not allow time for children to talk about anything not on her agenda. There was no time to mourn the geranium. Many seemingly small events can be enormously important for a child – losing a tooth, falling out with a friend, not understanding what others are doing. In allowing time to report, reflect and discuss, we are showing that learning is about life and what is important in life. The concerns of the learner are equally as important as the concerns of the teacher, and we need to find out what these are.

One way to check on children before they start a learning activity is to provide opportunities for comment, for example, by asking: 'Is there anything anyone wants to say before we start?' 'Are there any problems?' A problem shared is not always a problem halved, but when people are involved together in finding a solution to a problem they are more likely to find a solution and to accept responsibility for making the solution work.

In leading a group or class through a step-by-step process of problem-solving, it may be helpful to recall the teaching cycle of Romance-Generalisation-Precision advocated by Whitehead). In identifying the problem try to get the children to identify with the problem or an aspect of the problem, to embed it in their own human experience by an act of imagination, by making them part of the story. The following task presents one problem and process for group problem-solving.

Task 42

Reviewing a problem

Give the group of children a problem to solve.

Ask them:

1 What is the problem – whose problem is it, why is it a problem?
2 What are the possible solutions?
3 What are the best solutions?
4 How will we implement their solutions?
5 How will they find out if they work?

Sample problem: *Bullying*

Older children are reported to be bullying younger children in the play-ground. How will the group try to solve the problem?

One step-by-step process would be:

a) identifying the problem – by getting group members to remember or imagine how they felt when they were young and were picked on by older children

b) generating solutions – brainstorm in groups ideas for bringing bullying to an end, and list them

c) choosing the best options – ask each group to select three best ideas, compile a class list of ideas, discuss and vote on the best ideas to solve the problem

d) implementing the solutions – discuss how to translate good ideas into practice

e) testing the solutions – what are the criteria for success, who will judge, how and when?

A good time to reinforce the sense of community in the classroom is at the end of a learning activity. This can be done through a process of group review (see Chapter 9) by asking questions.

- What did you/we do in this lesson? (Show and tell.)
- What have you learnt?
- What did you like about this activity?
- What did you not like about this lesson?
- How should we continue what we have been doing?

Another strategy is 'last words', which is to ask all the group to have a turn, if they wish, to say something about the topic that they have not had the chance of saying. During this time no one must interrupt or respond. It is simply a time when each member has one, and only one, chance to say a few last words before the session ends.

Creating a learning community in the school

Research into creating learning environments in school, is building the foundations for a systematic approach to improving the effectiveness of schools.[2] Its findings give teachers and schools clues as to what they should focus on in improving their schools and their students' chances of success.

One of the keys to school effectiveness identified by Mortimore is 'intellectually challenging teaching'. There seems to be a link between effective schools and those teaching and learning strategies which focus on challenging and developing thinking.

The growing emphasis on school effectiveness and school improvement reflects general concerns about the working of organisations that have concerned managers and politicians over the last three decades. This has coincided with times of tremendous change for both business organisations and schools. Studies of how effective organisations cope with change, what makes for excellence, and how successful organisations relate to their customers and workforce have identified three key factors:[3]

- the quality of planning within the organisation
- the nature of the culture within the organisation
- the ability of organisations to focus on their key functions.

These match well with what research has identified as the three issues central to the success of schools – development planning, school ethos and quality in teaching and learning.

Over recent years there has been a change of climate in the expectations held of schools. The growing research evidence that schools make a difference has done much to dispel the pessimism of the 1960s and 1970s. Schools had, for a decade or more, been charged by social critics with a cultural conservatism that perpetuated and exaggerated social inequalities. Schools could not counter the effects of class and culture. Some radical critics argued that real education could only be achieved outside of the school system.

Pioneering research in the late 1970s by Rutter et al.[4] demonstrated that some schools were more effective than others, and that there was a school effect. By comparing students on entry and on leaving school, they developed the concept of added value, which is the educational benefit to the child specifically provided by the school over a period of time.

Studies of secondary schools by Rutter identified some common characteristics in effective schools, which he called 'process characteristics', and these factors have been largely confirmed in subsequent studies in this country and abroad. These factors, in order of importance are:

- leadership
- school climate
- teacher-pupil relationship
- quality of curriculum/teaching
- pupil socio-economic background
- evaluation
- financial resources
- physical characteristics.

Researchers found strong links between some of these features, especially between the most consistent factors such as leadership and school climate, pupil-teacher relationships and learning/teaching. There has been much debate on criteria and research methods used to assess achievement, but the central question: 'Are some schools more effective than others?' has clearly been answered. Research studies have tended to find that effective schools are likely to be effective for everyone in them. Current research is now probing questions related to the complexities and differences between schools and within schools. For example, are there differential effects between classes in one school, or even within the same classroom?

Researchers have begun to take an interest in 'moving schools', a term taken from business management to indicate dynamic and developing schools, as opposed to 'stuck' or declining schools. Research has supported what many teachers have found from experience – that there can be good teachers in 'stuck' or declining schools, and in 'rump' groups or departments left behind in developing schools. It is clear that effective proponents of change need to value individual differences and be sensitive to the needs of teachers in a time of change. It is also clear that the richest culture for change is one in which everyone has something to gain and where all teachers, parents and pupils are involved in learning.

Improving schools

The effective school is an improving school. Disraeli once said: 'In a perfect man change is constant'. We might rewrite this to read 'in a perfect school change is constant'. However, it is the quality of change that is the key, and the way that change affects every individual and aspect of the school. The three key areas that relate to effectiveness and improvement are:

- school development planning
- ethos
- teaching and learning.

School development planning

School development planning is the enabling mechanism whereby schools can adopt a planned approach to change and improvement. Schools, in many European countries, and in Australia, Canada and the USA, are being required or encouraged to create a rolling programme of school development plans. The school improvement process has been likened to a journey, planning becomes the means of transport to the destination, and the plan is the map for the journey. One of the dangers is that of the map becoming the destination. School improvers need to beware of planning being a mere pen-and-paper exercise.

Improvements within the classroom depend on improvements outside the classroom. School development planning must focus on 'the total school', so that all elements that are important to teachers, governors, parents and pupils are included. Important elements of development planning include:

- process *the focus of planning, the planning team, the planning programme*
- ownership *the widest participation and collaboration in the process, negotiated outcomes*
- evaluation *agreement on why and how the plan is to be monitored and assessed.*

There are two questions that can be asked about any plan.

- Does the plan support the aims and ethos of the school?
- Does the plan result in improvements in learning, teaching and attainment of pupils?

School ethos

One consistent finding of research into effective schools is that 'ethos' is an important ingredient. Ethos is defined as the climate of the school, and is expressed in the organisational conditions and web of personal relationships within the school. Ethos and school culture is difficult to define. It is the outward expression of the 'secret harmonies' of the school, those norms, beliefs and values which become modes, standards and rules of operation. As one inspector put it: 'It's what you feel in your bones about a school when you have been in it for some time'. It is clear from research that there is something intangible about a school, a style, tone and atmosphere that affects pupil performance. An effective school has a positive ethos, reflected in a range of factors that include:

- a sense of identity and pride in the school *good schools have a sense of cohesion*
- a welcoming environment *good schools present themselves in positive ways*
- high pupil and teacher expectations *good schools expect the best of people*
- strong and purposeful leadership *good schools are well managed*
- positive attitudes towards pupils *good schools motivate pupils through praise*
- work in partnership with parents and the community *good schools involve others.*

One way in which schools can identify actions needed to enhance their ethos is to conduct an ethos survey – to ask pupils, teachers and parents what they think of the school and how it could be improved. Examples of ways to improve school ethos might include developing opportunities for extra-curricular activities, encouraging parents and members of the community to involve themselves in school activities, or providing reward systems in which all pupils can benefit. Indicators of success in developing school ethos might include pupil achievement in academic and non-academic pursuits, better attendance, more time on task in the classroom, more investment in homework, and perceptions of better teacher-pupil relationships.

Improving teaching and learning

Good schools are said to be 'learner centred', 'learning enriched' and a 'learning community'; one in which adults as well as students are engaged in life-long learning, dedicated to the growth of individuals and the realisation of human potential. Research, however, highlights a tension between the needs of the individual as learner, and the job of the teacher to cater for the many and simultaneous dimensions of learning in the classroom. In looking at improving teaching and learning we need to look at what teachers do and what learners do, and the critical relationship between the two.

Research highlights the differences in learning style and developmental needs of students. Classroom teachers and school policies will seek maximise learning opportunities for individuals in different ways, for example, by providing opportunities for:

- independent learning *where the pupil's relationship is primarily with learning resources*
- supported learning *where the relationship is primarily between learner and teacher* (see Chapter 8)
- peer learning *where there is a learning/teaching relationship between pupils in pairs and groups*
- extended learning *supported learning out of school, including homework and home study.*

We know that effective teachers exhibit an impressive range of competencies, including *curriculum knowledge* (the content of teaching); *pedagogical knowledge* (the skills of teaching in theory and application) that includes the skills of presentation, organisation and management of learning; psychological knowledge of children as individuals; and sociological knowledge of the nature of cultural and social groups. In addition, they need *evaluative skills* to assess children's learning and the effectiveness of their own teaching. Effective teaching is a complex activity which needs not only the professional skills mentioned, but also personal qualities such as imagination, creativity and sensitivity to stimulate, support and encourage learning. We know that even this list, however, is not sufficient to guarantee learning. Determined pupils can and do resist even the most skilled of teachers. Learning can also take place in the absence of effective teaching. However, the best results are likely to occur when there is a match between effective teaching and learning.

How can we tell when there is effective teaching and learning? The following are some indicators.

Student outcomes

- achievement *evidence of progress and achievement*
- ethos *general attitudes to school and learning*
- self-concept *measures of self-concept and motivation as learners*
- behaviour *measures of improved behaviour*
- attendance *good attendance/truancy measures*
- further education *measures of post-school progress.*

Teacher/school outcomes

- ethos *survey of attitudes to school/teaching*
- professional development *survey of teacher as learner/extended professional study*
- staff absence
- quality of teaching *student outcomes and relationships*
- assessment *monitoring student progress and self-evaluation.*

A key lesson from school effectiveness research is that the ends – outcomes in terms of effective teaching and learning – must always be kept in sight. Schools must always keep in sight their primary purpose, and while keeping a keen eye on the internal challenge both to maintain what is good and to strive for the better, they should also look at the example of other successful schools.

Effective schools – places where children succeed

Research reports into over 700 primary and secondary schools identified as excellent, in the USA, were published by Research for Better Schools (USA, 1987–8). Its authors analysed the qualities and characteristics that are common to effective primary schools and effective primary school teaching. Questions arise of course: What constitutes success? How can successful schools be identified? How can you compare schools serving different communities? In this study, the schools were identified against various criteria of quality. The schools identified came from a variety of social settings, and the conclusions turn out to be surprisingly similar to other studies researching into school effectiveness, such as Peter Mortimore's junior school project.[5] From this research two lessons are clear.

- excellence can be achieved anywhere – in urban, suburban and rural schools, in schools varying in size, from 40 to over 1000 pupils, in both streamed and unstreamed schools
- themes that work are within the reach of all schools.

Research into effective schools identifies as indicators of quality and effectiveness the following ten elements:

- teaching that develops competence and character
- setting high expectations, monitoring standards and rewarding results
- having school leadership
- having clear goals and core values
- creating a professional work environment
- having positive student-teacher relationships
- having the resources to facilitate teaching and learning
- working in the community
- solving problems
- being unique.

Teaching that develops competence and character

Good schools combine effective teaching (clear goals, a broad but rigorous curriculum, and capable committed teachers) with successful socialisation of students (characterised by positive behaviour, good work habits and a commitment to the school community). Teachers had clearly focused views on the needs of their children. The most frequently mentioned needs were:

- basic skills – 87 per cent
- higher order thinking skills – 32 per cent

- self-esteem and personal development – 31 per cent
- good citizenship/preparation for adult life – 31 per cent.

In effective schools resources and programmes vary. What is common is teachers who work hard to provide active and intellectually challenging teaching in a warm, supportive environment.

Setting high expectations, monitoring standards and rewarding results

Good teachers and good schools set and communicate high expectations of academic performance and behaviour. Successful schools believe that all pupils can be motivated to learn. They are characterised by intensive care and strong reward or recognition systems. They make increased demands on their pupils, but they balance this with increased recognition for success, for example, in formal year achievement assemblies, and informal use of congratulatory messages to pupils and parents.

To be maintained these standards must be monitored and reinforced by appropriate rewards. The dilemma is that you cannot hold uniformly high expectations of all students. Good teachers work to overcome this by maintaining high standards for their classes over the long run, while, in the short term, varying their expectations for individual students, motivating their best work and recognising their achievements.

School leadership

Effective leadership is essential for school success. Dynamic leadership often stems from the head, but usually is shared with other professionals in school. There is no one style or formula for effective leadership. The best leaders adapt to their local school context. They:

- set and maintain a clear direction, articulating a vision or mission for the school
- facilitate the work of staff, with policies and programmes that support professional work
- model commitment to a collective focus on the goals and standards of the school.

There is not just one leader. Leadership in good schools is dispersed. Good leaders develop other leaders and create leadership teams where many individuals take leadership roles. Good leaders link strong monitoring control, with collective responsibility and a maximising of individual autonomy (similarly good teachers do this in the classroom).

Clear goals and core values

A shared purpose is achieved by agreeing common goals. These are given clarity by being written down and shared with all in the community – teachers, students, parents and local community. School success comes from vision linked to action. The shared purposes must be taken seriously and translated into action. Such a vision can form the basis for decisive action and the creation of a shared moral order. Establishing priorities will help to give them clear identity and can strengthen loyalty.

Creating professional work environments

Good schools share a collective sense of control. Individuals do not feel isolated, there is a sense of community, a satisfaction from being part of the group and school. This is achieved by maintaining the right balance of control and freedom. Seven elements are identified in the research as contributing to developing good people and a good environment:

- a sense of belonging
- a respect for teaching and for teachers
- a sense of control over the job
- support for personal and professional development
- care for the physical condition of the school
- recognition for effort
- reward for achievement.

Effective schools aim to raise the professional status of their teachers. They do this by increasing teachers' decision-making responsibilities and by creating good working conditions. This, in turn, is reflected in high staff attendance and low staff turnover. A sense of community and common purpose is fostered by making group involvement a priority in decision-making, building in planning time, and in showing appreciation of good work.

Positive student-teacher relationships

Successful schools and classes are characterised by students who try harder and show greater effort. They are well motivated. How is this achieved? Students are motivated through formal and informal relationships. In many of these schools, teachers and students are given opportunities to meet informally, for example, through extra-curricular activities, or through use of libraries, computer centres or other facilities in their free time, or in time when they can seek out a teacher for personal assistance. In some schools, each department has a work/resource centre open to students outside class time. In others, each student has a personal tutor who follows their career (about 10–15 students per tutor) and supports their progress through school. Good schools tend to work on being caring schools. One way they do this is to use their resources to provide lower pupil/teacher ratios and more pupil/teacher contact.

Resources to facilitate teaching and learning

Adequate resources, and the use of resources for the maximum effect can make a big difference to a school. Vital resources include:

- time *maximum use should be made of classroom learning time, with few interruptions, non-teaching activity reduced to a minimum, and time on learning tasks maximised*
- space *good schools and teachers try to use every available space for learning purposes*
- voluntary *help good schools have active voluntary help programmes to support teaching and learning.*

Working in the community

Good schools are characterised by high degrees of parental and community involvement. Two keys to community links are:

- a broad definition of community to include neighbours, local businesses, other service organisations, senior citizens and any others willing to help the school and its children
- strong communication links including home/school, pre-school and post-school links, with regular letters from staff summarising goals/achievements, previewing studies and informing news and needs. These links are pursued with energy, sincerity and seriousness, and are seen not as window-dressing, but as a critical element in school success.

Elements of working with the community include human resources, such as voluntary help in clerical duties, to tutor, help with, plan and implement activities. Many schools have active volunteer programmes, such as a 'grand-people programme', for non-parents and the retired, to help with groups or with specific subject skills, or as consultants. Public relations helps develop community links through strong PTAs, informative newsletters, sponsorship and fund-raising. Community service is shown by the way the schools invite themselves into the community to share and to serve. These, and other ways, help to build the identity of the school and affirm its core values.[3]

Solving problems

A characteristic of all schools, is that they have problems – obstacles to success. These may include inadequate facilities, inadequate funding, poor discipline, low attendance, falling rolls, complacency, drug abuse, low standards, poor school spirit, poor community relations and so on. Successful schools try to identify their problems and search aggressively for solutions, for example, in short 'target sessions' fifteen minutes before school to discuss a problem student. They tend to be solution-focused rather than problem-focused.

The path to excellence is strewn with obstacles. There is an underlying need for stubbornness and commitment in the face of problems, an unwillingness to accept defeat or mediocrity, not settling for good enough but seeking to do better. This involves not just talking about action, but a 'can do' philosophy showing itself in a willingness to do some positive problem-solving.

Being unique

Excellent schools, like excellent teachers, are all different. They all have their own unique characteristics, indeed they often strive to achieve uniqueness. They are innovative and open to change while holding fast to the core of their vision and values. They are responsive to those whom they serve. They value what is special about their learning community. They have a bias for action, for getting on with the job, but they like to do it in their own way. They have the capacity to renew vitality and performance. They use informed opportunism to allow for a flexibility in planning, to make the most of 'happy accidents'. They have a commitment to teaching and to the peculiarities of their school and of the team working within it.

Task 43

Creating a learning environment
What goals or outcomes do you want for your students?
1 How are they communicated?
2 Who knows them?
3 When are they reviewed?
Identify up to 7 (plus or minus 2) characteristics of the learning environment that you wish to create.
List these characteristics in order of importance.

The evidence of this research shows that successful schools do not necessarily have new approaches. What they do have are high levels of awareness of, and participation in, strategies that are tried and tested and that work. It is an incomplete picture with many pieces missing, but the themes here reflect the general conclusions arising from research literature. Specific policies and practices may be less important than the standards accepted by teachers and students and the general ethos that unites them into a caring community. From a working consensus about the purpose of education, comes a clarity of intent and, from this, all else (including a sense of pride and commitment) can follow. Research shows that there is no single or simple answer, no one solution or magic formula. Success comes from the chemistry of all the small positive things that count, blended by the uniqueness of the teacher and school in different ways to create places where children succeed.

A powerful learning environment in home, or school provides a continuity of purpose, and a stable and supportive framework where students are encouraged to think, question, discuss and map their ideas, to be divergent, to work with others, to respond to coaching, to review and their progress. As one child wrote about their ideal school: 'It is a place where you are encouraged to be yourself. They expect the best of you, and you feel at home there. It is a place you can always return to in your mind.' It is a place that lives in the present, but looks to the future. In the words of Kahlil Gibran:[6]

Your children are not your children.
They are the sons and daughters of life's longing for itself.
They come through you but not from you,
And though they are with you yet they belong not to you.
You may give them your love but not your thoughts.
You may house their bodies but not their souls,
For their souls dwell in the house of tomorrow, which you cannot visit, not in
  your dreams.
You may strive to be like them, but seek not to make them like you.
For life goes not backward nor tarries with yesterday.
You are bows from which your children as living arrows are sent forth.
The archer sees the mark upon the path of the infinite, and he bends you with his
might that his arrows may go swift and far.
Let your bending in the archer's hand be for gladness.
For even as he loves the arrow that flies, so he loves also the bow that is stable.

References

1   Gibbs, J. (1987) *Tribes: A Process for Social Development and Co-operative Learning*, Centre Source Publications, Santa Rosa, Cal.
2   Important books that summarise research into school effectiveness and improvement include:
    Corcoran, T. B. and Wilson, W. L. (1987) *Places Where Children Succeed: A Profile of Outstanding Elementary Schools*, Research for Better Schools Publications, Philadelphia, Penn.;
    Corcoran, T. B. and Wilson W. L. (1988) *The Search for Successful Secondary Schools*, Research for Better Schools Publications, Philadelphia, Penn.;
    Fullan, M. (1991) *The New Meaning of Educational Change*, Cassell, London;
    Mortimore, P. (1993) 'School Effectiveness and the Management of Effective Teaching, and Learning', *School Effectiveness and School Improvement*, vol. 4, no. 4, pp. 290–310;
    Mortimore, P. et al. (1988) *School Matters: The Junior Years*, Open Books, Wells;
    Reynolds, D. and Cuttance, P. (1992) *School Effectiveness: Research, Policy and Practice*, Cassell, London;
    Reynolds, D., Hopkins, D. and Stoll, L. (1993) 'Linking School Effectiveness Knowledge and School Improvement Practice: Towards a Synergy', *School Effectiveness and School Improvement*, vol. 4, no. 1, pp. 37–58;
    Rutter, M. et al. (1979) *Fifteen Thousand Hours: Secondary Schools and their Effects on Children*, Open Books, Wells;
    Tizard, B. et al. (1988) *Young Children in School in the Inner City*, Lawrence Erlbaum Associates, Hillsdale, New Jersey;
    OFSTED (1994) Improving Schools, HMSO, London.
3   See: Handy, C. (1990) *The Age of Unreason*, Business Books, Random Century, London;
    Peters, T. and Waterman, R. H. (1982) *In Search of Excellence*, Harper & Row, London;
    Peters, T. (1987) *Thriving on Chaos*, Macmillan, London;
    Kennedy, C. (1991) *Guide to the Management Gurus*, Business Books, Random Century, London;
    Senge, P. (1992) *The Fifth Discipline: The Art and Practice of the Learning Organisation*, MIT Press, Boston, Mass.;
    Peters, T. (1994) *The Tom Peters' Seminar: Crazy Times Call for Crazy Organisations*, Vintage, Random House, New York.
4   Rutter et al. (1979) op. cit.
5   Mortimore P. et al , op. cit.
6   Gibran, K. (1926, 1964 edn) *The Prophet*, Heinemann, London.

Bibliography

Adey, P. and Shayer, M. (1994) *Really Raising Standards*, Routledge, London.

Arnold, H. (1983) *Listening to Children Reading*, Hodder & Stoughton, London.

Ashman, A. and Conway, R. (1993) *Using Cognitive Methods in the Classroom*, Routledge, London.

Alexander, P. (1992) *Policy and Practice in Primary Education*, Routledge, London.

Amabile, T. M. (1983) *The Social Psychology of Creativity*, Springer-Verlag, New York.

Andrews, R., Costello, P. and Clarke, S. (1993) *Improving the Quality of Argument*, University of Hull, Hull, pp. 5–16.

Ausubel, D. (1968) *Educational Psychology: A Cognitive View*, Holt, Rinehart & Winston, London.

Bandura, A. (1977) *Social Learning Theory*, Prentice Hall, Englewood Cliffs, New Jersey.

Barell, J. (1991) *Teaching for Thoughtfulness*, Longman, Harlow.

Baron, J. and Sternberg, R. (1987) *Teaching Thinking Skills: Theory and Research*, W. H. Freeman, New York.

Bloom, B. and Krathwohl, D. R. (1956) *Taxonomy of Educational Objectives, Handbook 1: Cognitive Domain*, David McKay, New York.

Brandes, D. and Ginnis, P. (1986) *A Guide to Student-Centred Learning*, Blackwell, Oxford.

Bridges, D. (1979) *Education, Democracy and Discussion*, NFER, Windsor.

Buzan, T. (1974) *Use Your Head*, BBC Publications, London.

Clarke, J. (1990) *Patterns of Thinking: Integrating Learning Skills in Content Teaching*, Allyn & Bacon, Boston, Mass.

Corcoran, T. B. and Wilson, W. L. (1987) *Places Where Children Succeed: A Profile of Outstanding Elementary Schools*, Research for Better Schools Publications, Philadelphia.

Corcoran, T. B. and Wilson, W. L. (1988) *The Search for Successful Secondary Schools*, Research for Better Schools Publications, Philadelphia.

Costa, A. L. (ed.) (1991) *Developing Minds: A Resource Book for Teaching Thinking*, ASCD, Alexandra, Virginia.

Cowie, H., and Ruddock, J. (1988) *Co-operative Groupwork: An Overview*, BP Education Service, London.

de Bono, E. (1987) *CoRT Thinking Programme*, Science Research Associates, Henley.

Dillon, J. T. (1994) *Using Discussion in Classrooms*, Open University Press, Buckingham.

Doise, W. and Mugny, G. (1984) *The Social Development of the Intellect*, Pergamon, Oxford.

Doyle, R. (1986) *Webbing as a Prewriting Strategy*, Maryland Writing Project, Baltimore.

Edelman, G. (1992) *Bright Air, Brilliant Fire*, Penguin, Harmondsworth.

Edwards, D. and Mercer, N. (1987) *Common Knowledge: The Development of Understanding in the Classroom*, Methuen, London.

Feuerstein, R. (1980) *Instrumental Enrichment: An Intervention Program for Cognitive Modifiability*, Scott, Foresman & Company, Glenview, Ill.

Fisher, R. (ed.) (1987) *Problem-Solving in Primary Schools*, Blackwell, Oxford.

Fisher, R. and Vince, A. (1989) *Investigating Maths*, Blackwell/Simon & Schuster, Hemel Hempstead.

Fisher, R. (1990) *Teaching Children to Think*, Blackwell/Simon & Schuster, Hemel Hempstead.

Fisher, R. (1991) *Teaching Juniors*, Blackwell/Simon & Schuster, Hemel Hempstead.

Fisher, R. (1991) *Recording Achievement in Primary Schools*, Blackwell, Oxford.

Fisher, R. and Garvey, J. (1992) *Investigating Technology*, Simon & Schuster, Hemel Hempstead.

Fisher, R. and Alldridge, A. (1994) *Active PE*, Simon & Schuster, Hemel Hempstead.

Fisher, R (1994) *Active Art: A Primary Art Course*, Simon & Schuster, Hemel Hempstead.

Foote, H. C., Morgan, M. J. and Shute, R. H. (eds) (1990) *Children Helping Children*, Wiley, London.

Friedman, S. I., Scholnik, E. K. and Cocking, R. R. (eds) (1990) Blueprints for Thinking: *The Role of Planning in Cognitive Development*, Cambridge University Press, Cambridge.

Fullan, M. (1991) *The New Meaning of Educational Change*, Cassell, London.

Gage, N. L. (1968) *Explorations of the Teacher's Effectiveness in Explaining*, Stanford University, Stanford, Connecticut.

Galton, M. and Williamson, J. (1992) *Group Work in the Primary Classroom*, Routledge, London.

Gardner, H. (1983) *Frames of Mind: A Theory of Multiple Intelligence*; (1985) *The Mind's New Science: A History of the Cognitive Revolution*; (1988) The Unschooled Mind; (1982) *Art, Mind and Brain: A Cognitive Approach to Creativity*; (1993) *Creating Minds*, Basic Books, New York.

Garner, R. (1987) *Metacognition and Reading Comprehension*, Ablex, Norwood, New Jersey.

Gibbs, J. (1987) *Tribes: A Process for Social Development and Co-operative*

Learning, Centre Source Publications, Santa Rosa, Cal.

Gibran, K. (1926, 1964 edn) *The Prophet*, Heinemann, London.

Gould, P. and White, R. (1986) *Mental Maps*, (2nd edn), Allen & Unwin, London.

Gordon, W. J. J. (1961) *Synectics*, Harper & Row, London.

Graves, D. (1983) *Writing*, Heinemann, London.

Handy, C. (1990) *The Age of Unreason*, Business Books, Random Century, London.

Harri-Augstein, S. and Thomas, L. (1991) *Learning Conversations*, Routledge, London.

Harlen, W. (1993) *Teaching and Learning Primary Science*, Paul Chapman, London.

Hohmann, M., Banet, B. and Weikart, D. P. (1979) *Young Children in Action: A Manual for Pre-School Educators*, High Scope Education Research Foundation, Ypsilanti, Michigan.

Johnson, G., Hill, B. and Tunstall, P. (1992) *Primary Records of Achievement*, Hodder, London.

Kagan, S. (1988), *Co-operative Learning: Resources for Teachers*, University of California, Cal.

Kerry, T. (1982) *Effective Questioning*, Macmillan, London.

Kingston Friends Workshop Group (1985) *Ways and Means: An Approach to Problem-Solving*, Friends Meeting House, 78 Eden Street, Kingston, Surrey.

Langer, E. (1989) *Mindfulness*, Addison-Wesley, New York.

Lawrence, D. (1988) *Enhancing Self-Esteem in the Classroom*, Paul Chapman, London.

Luria, A. R. (1973) *The Working Brain*, Penguin, Harmondsworth; (1980) *Higher Cortical Functions in Man* (2nd edn), Basic Books, New York.

Luria, A. R. and Yudovich, F. A. (1971) *Speech and the Development of Mental Processes in the Child*, Penguin, Harmondsworth.

Meadows, S. and Cashdan, M. (1988) *Helping Children Learn: Contributions to a Cognitive Curriculum*, David Fulton, London.

Miller, G. A. (1956) 'The Magical Number Seven Plus or Minus Two: Some Limits on Our Capacity for Processing Information', *Psychological Review*, vol. 63.

Morgan, N. and Saxton J. (1991) *Teaching, Questioning and Learning*, Routledge, London.

Mortimore, P. et al. (1988) *School Matters*, Open Books, Wells.

Novak, J. D. and Gowin, D. B. (1984) *Learning How to Learn*, Cambridge University Press, Cambridge.

Papert, S. (1980) Mindstorms: *Children, Computers and Powerful Ideas*, Basic Books, New York.

Perkins, D. (1981) *The Mind's Best Work*, Harvard University Press, Cambridge, Mass.

Perkins, D. (1994) *The Intelligent Eye: Learning to Think by Looking at Art*, Getty Centre for Education in the Art, Santa Monica, Cal.

Peters, T. and Waterman, R. H. (1982) *In Search of Excellence*, Harper & Row, London.

Peters, T. (1987) *Thriving on Chaos*, Macmillan, London.

Peters, T. (1994) *The Tom Peters' Seminar: Crazy Times call for Crazy Organisations*, Vintage, Random House, New York.

Piaget, J. (1948/1974) *To Understand is to Invent: The Future of Education*, Viking, New York.

Reason, R. (1991) *Co-operating to Learn and Learning to Co-operate*, University College, London.

Resnick, L. (1987) *Education and Learning to Think*, National Academy Press, Washington, D.C.

Reynolds, D. and Cuttance, P. (1992) *School Effectiveness: Research, Policy and Practice*, Cassell, London.

Richardson, R. (1990) *Daring to be a Teacher*, Trentham Books, Stoke-on-Trent.

Rutter, M. et al. (1979) *Fifteen Thousand Hours: Secondary Schools and their Effects on Children*, Open Books, Wells.

Schwartz, R. and Parks, S. (1994) *Infusing the Teaching of Critical and Creative Thinking into Elementary Instruction*, Critical Thinking Press, Pacific Grove, Cal.

Scott, P. (1987) *A Constructivist View of Teaching and Learning in Science*, University of Leeds, Leeds.

Sternberg, R. J. (1988) *The Nature of Creativity*, Cambridge University Press, Cambridge.

Senge, P. (1992) *The Fifth Discipline: The Art and Practice of the Learning Organisation*, MIT Press, Boston, Mass.

Tharp, R. G. and Gallimore, R. (1988) *Rousing Minds to Life: Teaching, Learning, and Schooling in Social Context*, Cambridge University Press, Cambridge.

Tizard, B. and Hughes, M. (1984) *Young Children Learning*, Fontana, London.

Tizard, B. et al. (1988) *Young Children in School in the Inner City*, Lawrence Erlbaum Associates, Hillsdale, New Jersey.

Torrance, E. P. (1962) *Guiding Creative Talent*, Prentice Hall, Englewood Cliffs, New Jersey; (1965) *Rewarding Creative Behaviour*, Prentice Hall, Englewood Cliffs, New Jersey.

Underwood, D. M., and Underwood, G. (1990) *Computers and Learning: Helping Children Acquire Thinking Skills*, Blackwell, Oxford.

van Ments, M. (1990) Active Talk: *The Effective use of Discussion in Learning*, Kogan Page, London.

von Oech, Roger (1983) *A Whack on the Side of the Head*, Warner Books, London; (1987) *A Kick in the Seat of the Pants*, HarperCollins, London.

Vygotsky, L. S. (1962) *Thought and Language*, MIT Press, Cambridge, Mass.; (1978) *Mind in Society*, Harvard University Press, Cambridge, Mass.

Wallach, M. A. and Kogan, N. (1965) *Modes of Thinking in Young Children*, Holt, Rinehart & Winston, London.

Wasserman, S. (1978) *Put Some Thinking in your Classroom*, Benefic Press, New York.

Wellman, H. M. (1990) *The Child's Theory of Mind*, MIT Press, Cambridge, Mass.

Wragg, E. R. (1993) *Questioning*, Routledge, London.

Wragg, E. C. and Brown, G. (1993) *Explaining*, Routledge, London.

Wray, D. (1994) *Literacy and Awareness*, UKRA/Hodder, London.

Index

able children 97, 111
achievement 129ff, 147, 149, 150
Allen, W. 113
analogy 84
argument 55, 82
assessment 26, 35, 48–9, 74–6, 79, 96, 103, 104, 113, 126, 134, 148
attention 111

Bacon, F. 15
Bennett, N. 97, 105, 106
Bloom, B. 4, 14
Bloom's taxonomy 18
brain/mind 52–4, 59, 134–5
brainstorming 63, 64–5, 77, 100, 104
Bruner, J. 1, 12, 17, 90, 105

CASE (Cognitive Acceleration through Science Education) 3, 14
circle time 141–3
coaching viii, 54, 107ff
cognitive apprenticeship 108ff
cognitive confusion 2
cognitive mapping viii, 57ff
cognitive research 13
cognitive structures 114–115, 122
Comenius 91
community of enquiry 13, 22, 43, 48, 51, 55
concept mapping 6, 57, 62ff, 114
concepts 58ff
conceptual confusion 2, 108
Confucius 107, 120
CoRT Thinking Programme 3–4, 76ff
creativity 74ff
curriculum
    knowledge 147
    research 12
    subjects 40, 118
cybernetics 120